SWU-NAP- 025

UNIFORMS OF RUSSIAN ARMY DURING THE NAPOLEONIC WAR VOL.20

UNDER THE REIGN OF ALEXANDER I
EMPEROR OF RUSSIA BETWEEN 1801 AND 1825
MILITARY EDUCATIONAL INSTITUTIONS, FLAGS & STANDARDS

From the Viskovatov's greatest work:
"Historical description of the clothing and
arms of the Russian Army"

English translation by Mark Conrad

SOLDIERSHOP PUBLISHING

AUTHOR

Aleksandr Vasilevich Viskovatov born 22 April (4 May New Style) 1804, died 27 February (11 March) 1858 in St. Petersburg, Russian military historian. He graduated from the 1st Cadet Corps and served in the artillery, the hydrographic depot of the Naval Ministry, and then in the Department of Military Educational Institutions. He mainly studied historical artifacts and the histories of military units. Viskovatov's greatest work was the Historical Description of the Clothing and Arms of the Russian Army.

PUBLISHING'S NOTE

NOTE ABOUT BOOK PRINTING BEFORE 1925

LICENSES COMMONS

ACKNOWLEDGEMENTS

A Special Thanks to NYPL and other institutions for their kindly permission to use some images of his archives, collections or books used in our book.

Title: **UNIFORMS OF RUSSIAN ARMY DURING THE NAPOLEONIC WAR VOL. 20**
Military educational institutions, flags & standards By A.V.Viskovatov. Serie edit by Luca S. Cristini. First edition by Soldiershop. August 2018 Cover & Art Design: Luca S. Cristini. Plates re-colorations by Anna Cristini.
ISBN code: 978-88-93273527

Published by Soldiershop publishing, via Orio 35/4 - 24050 Zanica (BG) ITALY. wwwsoldiershop.com

UNIFORMS OF
THE RUSSIAN ARMY
DURING THE
NAPOLEONIC WAR
VOL. 20

UNDER THE REIGN OF ALEXANDER I EMPEROR OF
RUSSIA BETWEEN 1801 AND 1825

*

MILITARY EDUCATIONAL INSTITUTIONS
FLAGS & STANDARDS

Russland.

Musketier.	Grenadier.	Grenadier.	Offiziere.
			Dienstanzug Ausgehanzug.

1812—1815.

▲ *Russian infantry soldiers*

HISTORICAL DESCRIPTION OF THE CLOTHING AND ARMS OF THE RUSSIAN ARMY - A.V. VISKOVATOV
(First English translation by Mark Conrad)

Soldiershop is glad to presents the complete collection of the great job made by A.V. Viskovatov dedicated to the uniforms and weapons belonging to the Russian army during the Napoleonic period, until 1825. The time we considered corresponds to the reigns of two Tzars: Paul I, who reigned since 1769 until his murder on the 23rd of March 1801, and his son Aleksandr Pavlovič Romanov, that with the title of Alexander I, sat on the throne until the 1st December 1825.

Our reprint in based on the original 19th century volumes, to be precise the volumes from 7 to 9 are dedicated to the reign of Paul I; this first part is distributed on 7 volumes, having a numbering from 1 to 7. From number 10 to 18 of the original volumes, the second part is dedicated to the Russian troops under Alexander I. These still being worked on and they will be soon ready, distributed on twenty volumes approximately. Our new edition, the first ever published in English, both on paper and digital format, boasts a large number of color plates, many of them unpublished and coloured by our team of expert artists and scholars of uniformology. Each volume is based on 50/70 plates, always accompanied by the original translated text which describes the uniforms, the organization and the armament of the Russian army of the period.

In this book we present the Russian military educational institutions, flags & standards of the Napoleonic wars. A unique work in its genre, a must have in any respecting collection!

Aleksandr Vasilevich Viskovatov born 22 April (4 May New Style) 1804, died 27 February (11 March) 1858 in St. Petersburg, Russian military historian. He graduated from the 1st Cadet Corps and served in the artillery, the hydrographic depot of the Naval Ministry, and then in the Department of Military Educational Institutions. He mainly studied historical artifacts and the histories of military units. Viskovatov's greatest work was the Historical Description of the Clothing and Arms of the Russian Army (Vols. 1-30, St. Petersburg, 1841-62; 2nd ed. Vols. 1-34, St. Petersburg - Novosibirsk - Leningrad, 1899-1948). This work is based on a great quantity of archival documents and contains four thousand colored illustrations.

Viskovatov was the author of Chronicles of the Russian Army (Books 1-20, St. Petersburg, 1834-42) and Chronicles of the Russian Imperial Army (Parts 1-7, St. Petersburg, 1852). He collected valuable material on the history of the Russian navy which went into A Short Overview of Russian Naval Campaigns and General Voyages to the End of the XVII Century (St. Petersburg, 1864; 2nd edition Moscow, 1946). Together with A.I. Mikhailovskii-Danilevskii he helped prepare and create the Military Gallery in the Winter Palace.

He wrote the historical military inscriptions for the walls of the Hall of St. George in the Great Palace of the Kremlin. (From the article in the Soviet Military Encyclopedia.)

CONTENTS

*

Preface pag. 5

RUSSIAN ARMY- MILITARY INSTITUTIONS
CHANGES IN THE UNIFORMS AND EQUIPMENT OF GUARDS GARRISON, INVALID,
EDUCATIONAL, FLAGS & STANDARDS OF REGULAR FORCES FROM 1801 TO 1825.

I. 1st, 2nd, and SHKLOV (from 1807 SMOLENSK, and from 1824 MOSCOW) CADET CORPS, IMPERIAL MILITARY ORPHANS HOME, and the NOBILIARY REGIMENT.

[1-i, 2-i i Shklovskii (c 1807 goda Smolenskii, a s 1824—Moskovskii) Kadetskie Korpusa, IMPERATORSKII Voenno-Sirotskii dom i Dvoryanskii polk.]

During the whole of EMPEROR ALEXANDER I's reign, the uniforms and arms of Military Educational Institutions [*Voenno-Uchebnyya Zavedeniya*] underwent, with small differences, all the changes that occurred in the army in general and which are described in detail in the preceding chapters of *Historical Description of the Clothing and Arms of Russian Army*.

9 April 1801 – Pupils in the 1st, 2nd, and Shklov Cadet Corps and the IMPERIAL Military Orphans Home were ordered to cut off their **curls** [*pukli*] and have **queues** [*kosy*] only 4 vershoks [7 inches] long, tying them midway down the collar [1].

21 July 1801 – Generals and field and company-grade officers of the above institutions were ordered to wear hats of a new pattern, completely identical to those introduced at this time in Army and Guards Infantry regiments [2].

In 1802 – *Cadets in the Grenadier companies* of the 1st and 2nd Cadet Corps were prescribed the same uniform clothing and weapons as were received on 30 April of this year by Grenadier and Musketeer regiments, namely:

Coat – with two rows of buttons, of dark-green cloth, with a red standing collar; red cuffs, cuff flaps, and skirt turnbacks; dark-green piping on the collar, cuffs, and cuff flaps; flat brass buttons; two shoulder straps: red in the 1st Cadet Corps and white in the 2nd; gold galloon sewn along the lower and side edges of the collar, along the upper edge of the cuffs, and along three sides of the cuff flaps (Illus. 2317, 2318, and 2319).

Forage cap – of dark-green cloth, with a band and tassel the same color as the collar, with piping on the seams in the same color as the shoulder straps.

Grenadier cap – almost the exact same pattern as under EMPEROR PAUL I, namely: with a brass front plate, three brass grenades behind and on the sides; on the plate, over almost its entire surface, was stamped a depiction of a two-headed Russian eagle with St. George on its breast; red top (the same color as collar and cuffs), but the rear or band the same color as the shoulder straps, i.e. red in the 1st Cadet Corps and white in the 2nd. The edging around the plate and below the band was black, as before. The trim on the top part was white cotton tape, while the pompons were white with a red center in the 1st Corps and red with a white center in the 2nd (Illus. 2317 and 2318).

Other items such as pants, boots, neckcloth, swords (with a short-sword blade), sword belts, swordknots, pouches, and musket were prescribed to be of the same patterns as in Grenadier regiments.

Grenadier non-commissioned officers were uniformed similarly to the other cadets but with only one shoulder strap, on the right shoulder, and with pompons on the grenadier cap in three colors: white, black, and orange, as was the *trinchik* or colored band on the swordknot. When in formation, they followed the example of non-commissioned officers in Grenadier regiments and were authorized gloves with cuffs, canes, muskets, and front pouches.

Cadets in musketeer companies had the same uniforms and arms as in Grenadier companies but with a three-cornered hat in place of the cap. The hat was exactly like those introduced at this time in Musketeer regiments, with tassels of the same colors as the pompons on grenadier caps. Instead of front pouches, regular cartridge pouches, while *non-commissioned officers* additionally had halberds instead of muskets, with straw-colored shafts (Illus. 2319).

Field and *company-grade officers* and *generals* had coats with collars, cuffs, and shoulder straps of the same colors as cadets, with narrow gold galloon along the edges of the shoulder straps and gold ring-shaped [*kol'tseobraznyi*] embroidery on the collar, cuffs, and cuff flaps. The remaining parts of the uniform, as well as weaponry, were for them the same for officers in Grenadier and Musketeer regiments, with the shafts of their spontoons being the same color as for halberds (Illus. 2320 and 2321).

Pupils [Vospitanniki] in the *Young Boys Section [Maloletnoe otdelenie]* at the 1st Cadet Corps wore single-breasted jackets without tails, and long pants: of dark-green cloth in fall, winter, and spring, and in summer—of linen [*kholstinnyi, ili iz flamskago polotna*], with covered buttons; dark-green forage caps with red bands and tassels; greased boots without buckles, and white stockings. They did not have neckclothes, but the shirt's white collar protruded over the jacket. When released from the building and the Corps grounds, they wore over the jacket a dark-green cloth single-breasted frock coat [*syurtuk*] with a narrow standing collar of red cloth, and instead of a forage cap they had black *kartuz* caps, rounded at the top, made from first-shear wool [*poyarkovyi*], with two flaps that tie together in front over the visor, with narrow woolen tape trim on the edge of these flaps and the visor. In winter, with the cloth jacket, or with the frock coat when allowed outside the Corps, young pupils had white chamois gloves with warm inserts [*varezhki*], sewn to the two ends of a long narrow multicolored ribbon which was thrown over behind the neck and then passed under the armpits. It was crossed at the back with one end over the other so that the gloves lay at waist level (Illus. 2322). During heavy frosts woolen *karpetki* (short socks) were worn.

Drummers and fifers had a coat without shoulder straps, with dark-green cloth swallows' nests at the shoulders, and had sewn-on tape, red with yellow checks. Drums were prescribed to be the of the same pattern as in Grenadier regiments, while drumsticks were straw colored (Illus. 2323).

Senior drummers [Barabannye starosty] (the corps drummers) and *musicians [muzykanty]* had the same uniforms as company drummers as well as the same distinctions as prescribed for these ranks in regiments of Army and Guards Infantry (Illus. 2323) [3].

19 October 1803 – All cadet **non-commissioned officers** were ordered to have two shoulder straps on their coats, like cadets, instead of one [4].

In 1803 generals, field-grade officers on the formation establishment, and adjutants in the 1st and 2nd Cadet Corps were authorized **shabracks** and **pistol carriers** of the patterns established this year for Grenadier and Musketeer regiments, dark green in color with red piping all around, with two rows of gold galloon, and with red cloth in the space between this galloon [5].

In 1804 – in the 1st and 2nd Cadet Corps grenadier caps and musketeer hats were replaced by cloth **headdresses** of the same pattern as used at this time in Guards Infantry regiments, with tassels and pompons of the same colors as were on the aforementioned caps and hats, and with gold galloon around the upper edge of the crown (Illus. 2324) [6]. In this year, for generals and company and field-grade officers of Military Educational Institutions, **hats** were introduced with a buttonhole loop of narrow gold galloon instead of embroidery, and with a high plume [7].

13 February 1805 – In the 1st and 2nd Cadet Corps, on the cadet **headdresses** in Grenadier companies, it was ordered that there be, above the visor, a brass grenade with a single flame, and a horsehair plume: for cadets—all black (Illus. 2325), non-commissioned officers—black with a white top with a yellow stripe down its center; drummers and fifers—red [8].

2 February 1806 – Officers' **spontoons** were withdrawn, and in their place when in formation they were ordered to use swords [*shpagi*] [9].

31 March 1806 – Cadet **non-commissioned officers** were ordered to have two rows of galloon on their headdresses, while plain cadets had one, as before [10].

28 July 1806 – Cadets were ordered to cut their **queues** off short, but generals and field and company-grade officers were, in this regard, allowed to proceed according to their own wishes [11].

17 February 1807 - Generals and field and company-grade officers were allowed to wear double-breasted uniform **frock coats** [*mundirnye syurtuki*] of dark-green cloth with red cloth collar and cuffs; dark-green piping on the collar and cuffs; red stamin lining and gilt buttons [12].

17 September 1807 - Generals and company and field-grade officers of Military Educational Institutions were ordered to wear **epaulettes** instead of shoulder straps, of the pattern established at this time for Grenadier regiments, but completely gold (Illus. 2326). From this same year on officers stopped wearing **queues** and continued to powder their hair only for grand parades and appearances at HIGHEST Court [13].

15 October 1807 – Cadets were ordered to not wear the **sword belt** around the waist, but over the right shoulder, under the cartridge-pouch belt, crosswise and the two belts being the same width. As consequence of this the seventh button under the coat's opening was abolished. Along with this, the sword belt as well as the crossbelt were prescribed to be stitched along the edges, and made with a slight bend so that the upper edges of both belts come closer to the collar. Bayonet scabbards with the new sword belts were placed in a frog to the right of the short sword, and worn parallel to it. This was all as introduced at this time in Army and Guards Infantry (Illus. 2327) [14].

23 December 1807- Cadets were given a new pattern of summer and winter (gray for everyday use and white at other times) **pants**, of the style confirmed at this time for infantry troops, i.e. the first with integral spats and covered buttons, and the second with leather trim or cuffs, with seven brass buttons (Illus. 2327). Company-grade officers in summer uniform were ordered to wear the same pants as cadets, but in winter—boots reaching up to the knee, without cutouts in back [15].

From 1807 on, officers and regular pupils of the **IMPERIAL Military Orphans Home** received uniforms and arms as for the 1st Cadet Corps, but without embroidery on officers' coats, with a red cloth field on officers' epaulettes instead of gold, and with galloon for non-commissioned officers. Underage [*maloletnye*] pupils had clothing as for the young boy cadets of that same corps [16].

26 January 1808— Generals of Military Educational Institutions at parades, on designated calendar days [*tabelnye dni*], and at troop formations in general, were ordered to wear the newly established **standard generals' coat** [*obshchii general-skii mundir*]. And with the corps coat when not on duty, they were to dark-green pants instead of white [17].

(Note: The description of the standard generals' coat is found below, in the section about general officers' uniforms.)

5 August 1808 – Cadets were given **shakos** [*kivera*] similar in form to the headdresses introduced in 1804, but lower in height, trimmed with polished black leather, with a similar visor sewn to the front, a black leather chinstrap buttoned on the left side to a brass button In front was a brass grenade with three flames. Pompons and plumes remained as before (Illus. 2328). It was ordered that cartridge pouches have the same grenade as on the shakos [18].

25 October 1808 – Canes for officers were abolished [19].

12 November 1808 - Field and company-grade officers of Military Educational Institutions, when not on duty, were allowed to wear dark-green cloth **pants** instead of white ones [20].

In November of 1808, for officers of the 2nd and Smolensk Cadet Corps and the IMPERIAL Military Orphans Home a new pattern of **gorget** was confirmed, similar to that introduced at this time in the Army Infantry, while officers of the 1st Cadet Corps kept the existing gorgets [21].

1 April 1809 – Cadets were ordered to have galloon on the top and side edges of the **collar**, rather than on the bottom and side edges (Illus. 2329) [22].

30 May 1809 - Noncommissioned officers' front **pouches** [*podsumki*] were replaced by pouches [*sumy*] of the same pattern as prescribed for cadets. privates. Drummers,fifers, and musicians were given shoulder straps on both shoulders [23].

8 June 1809 - The plumage on **generals' hats** was discontinued. The hat's former pattern of buttonhole was replaced with a new one made of four thick, twisted cords, of which the two middle ones were intertwined with each other as if in a plait [24].

11 June 1809 – **Shakos** were provided with cords: all white for cadets (Illus. 2329), and for non-commissioned officers and musicians—white with a mixture of black and orange [25].

6 December 1809 – When in formation, company-grade officers were ordered to have **shakos** of the same pattern as established for cadets, but with silver cords with a mixture of black and orange silk. Only the tassels and acorns were all silver. The shakos had the same additional distinctions as for officers' shakos in Army and Guards Infantry. These shakos were prescribed the same grenades, with three flames, as used by cadets, except gilded, and the same black plumes as cadets in Grenadier companies (Illus. 2329). Generals were not authorized shakos. At this same time all use of hair powder by officers was stopped [26].

In 1809 the **1st and 2nd Nobiliary Battalions**, newly formed at the 2nd Cadet Corps, were prescribed the exact same uniform clothing and weapons as for the 2nd Cadet Corps but without embroidery on officers' coats and with gold galloon only on the cuff flaps of nobles' coats. This did not extend to non-commissioned officers, who additionally had gallon on the collar and cuffs (Illus. 2330) [27].

10 July 1810 – Nobles (students in the **Nobiliary Regiment**) were ordered to have yellow **shoulder straps** on the coat instead of white (Illus. 2331) [28].

In 1810, for the 1st and 2nd Cadet Corps and the Nobiliary Regiment, a new pattern of **shako plate** was introduced in place of the grenade with three flames. This was in the form of a semicircle of radiance made up of matte and polished rays that were rounded at their tips. In the lower part was a semicircle with an impressed two-headed eagle. Along with this, cadets were ordered to have flat scales on their shako chinstraps, in the style for officers (Illus. 2332 and 2333) [29].

22 February 1811 – In place of their previous **shako plumes**, Grenadier platoons in the 1st and 2nd Cadet Corps and Nobiliary Regiment were given new ones of the pattern introduced at this time in Grenadier regiments. Non-commissioned officers, instead of multicolored shako cords, were ordered to have white ones, with only their bows and tassels having a mixture of black and orange colors (Illus. 2334) [30].

23 September 1811 – Students were given a new pattern of **forage cap**, dark-green with a red band, identical to those established at this same time for Grenadier regiments (Illus. 2335) [31].

Officers were ordered to have the same forage caps as cadets except with visors [32].

9 October 1811 – The **halberds** of cadet non-commissioned officers were withdrawn, and they were given muskets and pouches identical to those for cadets [33].

25 October 1811 – **Canes** were withdrawn from these same non-commissioned officers [34].

20 November 1811 – Non-commissioned officers' **gloves** with gauntlet cuffs were abolished [35].

In 1812 all ranks in Military Educational Institutions, except non-combatants, were given a new pattern of **shako**, lower than before, with a large spread or widening toward the top, and concave sides. Along with this the former high **collars**, diagonally open in front, were replaced by lower ones closed in front by small hooks and loops. Cadets' **pants cuffs** and officer **boots** were ordered to be high, up to the knee (Illus. 2336 and 2337).

From 1813 under-aged cadets' **forage caps** with tassels and their *kartuz* caps were replaced by round forage caps of dark-green cloth with a red band, of the pattern used by formation companies [36].

In 1814 the **cockades** on officers' hats, around which was a black ribbon with orange checks, were directed to have a second white ribbon (paper or silk) of the same width, which was latter replaced by a silver one. At the same time all musicians, fifers, and drummers were given double-breasted coats in place of single-breasted, closed in front with small hooks and loops, with sewn-on lace not just on one side of the front opening, but both (Illus. 2338) [37].

24 January 1816 - The **scabbards** for cadets' short swords [*tesaki*] and bayonets, and subsequently also for officers' swords [*shpagi*], were ordered to be black: the first polished and the last lacquered [38].

4 August 1817 – Officers were ordered to have **shako cords** that were completely silver, without any admixture of black and orange silk [39].

8 December 1817 - It was ordered that for lower ranks the **leather cuffs on cloth pants** were to have spat-like projections [*kozyr'ki*] of a pattern similar to the spats on summer pants.

From this year, cadets as well as officers in all Military Educational Institutions began to wear **shakos** higher than before, with a flat top and not concave as introduced in 1812, and students in the 1st and 2nd Cadet Corps were given multicolored shako bows and tassels, identical to those for non-commissioned officers (Illus. 2339) [40].

23 August 1818 – On **musicians' and drummers' coats** the shoulder pieces or wings were ordered to be red [41].

In 1818 – With the division of the **Smolensk Cadet Corps** into two formed [*stroevyya*] companies and an underage or Young Boys Section [*Maloletnee otdelenie*], the latter was prescribed the same clothing as the Young Boys Section of the 1st Cadet Corps and IMPERIAL Orphans Home, while the former received the same uniforms and arms as Musketeer companies of the Nobiliary Regiment, with only the cadets' yellow shoulder straps and officers' gold epaulette fields changed to white, and without gold galloon on the cuff flaps of cadets' coats [42]. (Note: All information regarding the previous uniforms of this Corps was destroyed by fire in 1812 when the city of Smolensk was occupied by the enemy.)

4 April 1819 - The **spats** on the leggings in use since 1817 were removed[43].

10 April 1919 – The **hornists**, or **signalers**, introduced onto the authorized strength of Military Educational Institutions were prescribed the same uniforms as company drummers, while signal horns were ordered to be of yellow brass with white straps, painted on the inside in red with a gold wreath around the edge (Illus. 2340) [44].

20 September 1820 – Officers of Military Educational Institutions, except the 1st Cadet Corps, were given a new pattern of **gorget**, identical to that received at this time by officers in Grenadier regiments. In this same year of 1820 there were changes in the coats of musicians, hornists, fifers, and drummers, consisting of the **sewn-on tape** being placed closer together, almost touching one another, and on the swallows' nests the tape was no longer perpendicular as before, but at a diagonal toward the lower edge. Also, the lower edge of the collar began to be also trimmed with this tape (Illus. 2341) [45].

10 March 1822 – Students in Musketeer companies were ordered to have round woolen **pompons** on their shakos, and officers—silver pompons (Illus. 2342) [46].

19 November 1823 – Students released from the grounds to their relatives in inclement and cold weather were ordered to wear **greatcoats** of the pattern for soldiers. Until this time they had been allowed to have their own greatcoats of the officers' pattern [47].

15 February 1824 – Students at Military Educational Institutions were ordered to not have leather cuffs on their gray everyday, or home [*domashnie*], **pants**, but rather have them only on the white pants (Illus. 2343) [48].

In 1824 – The **skirt tails** of students' coats, which up to this time had one covering the other, were to be cut so that their inner edges came together, and sewn together where they touched. To the decorative end [*trinchik*] of the **shako cords**, which was to be level with the right shoulder, was to be added a special loop of white cord attached to the button on the right shoulder strap (Illus. 2344). From this time, cadets as well as officers began to wear a shako higher than before, and shako cords that were wider than before (Illus. 2344), but specific rules for this have not been located [49].

II. NOBILIARY CAVALRY SQUADRON.[*Dvoryanskii kavaleriiskii eskadron.*]

28 November 1811 – Nobles in the *Nobiliary Cavalry Squadron*, established alongside the Nobiliary Regiment, were prescribed the same uniform coat as that regiment, while pants, gloves, helmets, pouches, broadswords, and boots with spurs were ordered to be of the same patterns as used in Army Dragoon regiments (Illus. 2345). Officers to instruct these nobles in the cavalry service were assigned from Cavalry regiments. Horses, with all saddlery and furniture, were provided to the squadron from Guards Cavalry regiments [50].

In 1812 – The **collars** on nobles' coats were ordered to be lower than before, without being diagonally open in front, and closed by means of small hooks [51].

20 May 1814 – Instead of double-breasted **coats**, the squadron's nobles were given single-breasted ones with nine flat brass buttons, red piping along the front opening and from the opening to the skirt tails. On helmets, instead of the previous plates depicting a two-headed eagle, it was ordered to have plates identical to those used in the 1st and 2nd Cadet Corps and Nobiliary Regiment [52].

14 August 1814 – Nobles were given **riding trousers** of gray cloth with two wide stripes and piping of the same color as the dress coat's collar, with leather along the inner seam [53].

12 December 1816 – The squadron's nobles were ordered to have: instead of round cuffs—slit cuffs, with two buttons on each, as before, red with dark-green piping; accouterments, arms, and horse furniture as for Army Dragoon regiments: saddle cloths the same color as the dress coat, with piping, trim, monogram, and crown the same color as the collar (Illus. 2346). Officers received the same uniform clothing with their prescribed distinctions that distinguished them from lower ranks (Illus. 2347) [54].

28 February 1817 – Officers of the Nobiliary Cavalry Squadron were ordered to have **pouches** of the pattern introduced at this time for officers of Army Dragoon regiments, with gold galloon on the crossbelt and silver buckle, clasp, end piece, prickers, and fine chains [55].

14 Marcy 1817- The squadron's **officers**, whether standing in formation or when wearing sashes, were ordered to be in dress coats with short tails and wearing pouches [56].

6 May 1817 – **Trumpeters** were ordered to have, on their coats, red wings instead of the previous dark green [57].

8 March 1818 – The squadron was given new **uniforms and weapons** as follows:

1) Instead of helmets, shakos identical to those used in the Nobiliary Regiment, but with red pompons and a white hair

plume. For nobles the hair at the base—and for non-commissioned officers at the top—of the plume was black with a thin scattering of orange mixed in.

2) Instead of yellow shoulder straps, woolen epaulettes of that same color, of the pattern used by Army Dragoon regiments.

3) Gold galloon on the cuffs, while the collar, as before, had no galloon, except for non-commissioned officers.

4) Instead of white pants with high boots—*chakchiry* pants of dark-green cloth with wide stripes and piping the same color as the collar, with one button at the bottom and sewn-on cuff reinforcements [*kragi*].

5) Instead of broadswords, sabers with a sword belt and hook identical to those introduced in Army Dragoon regiments. Officers were prescribed the same uniforms, along with their usual distinctions (Illus. 2348) [58].

In 1820 – The tape on **trumpeters' coats** began to be sewn on more closely together [59].

In 1824 – Nobles as well as officers began to wear a **shako** taller than before, with wider cords than previously, these being fastened to the button on the right epaulette by means of a special small loop [60].

III. MAIN ENGINEERING SCHOOL. [*Glavnoe inzhenernoe uchilishche.*]

24 November 1819 – Conductors [i.e. cadets, or students – M.C.] and officers on the establishment of the *Main Engineering School*, formed from the old Engineer School [*Inzhenernaya shkola*], kept their previous uniforms, with the following changes:

1) On conductors' shakos, instead of a grenade with a single flame, they were given tin plates of the pattern for Cadet Corps, with the addition of two axes in the plate's shield, under the eagle.

2) Cuff flaps of conductors' dress coats were ordered to be trimmed on three sides with silver galloon, after the pattern for Cadet Corps.

3) Conductors who distinguished themselves by their diligence and conduct were authorized to wear a silver sword knot on the short sword [*tesak*].

4) Accouterments and weapons were ordered to be of the same patterns as used in Sapper and Pioneer battalions.

5) Officers, when in formation, were ordered to wear shakos instead of hats, identical to conductors' shakos, while their coat embroidery was to be of the pattern for Cadet Corps, but silver instead of gold (Illus. 2349 and 2350) [61].

3 May 1820 – Conductors and unit officers [*stroevye ofitsery*] were ordered to have all-red **cuff flaps** on their dress coats, instead of dark green with red piping (Illus. 2351) [62].

25 January 1822 – Junkers and conductors in the Main Engineering School were given round **pompons** for their shakos, of red wool, but silver for unit officers (Illus. 2352) [63].

In 1824 – The changes indicated in the preceding description of **uniforms** for Cadet Corps and the Nobiliary Regiment were extended to the Main Engineering School, which received a shako that was taller than before, with cords that were wider (Illus. 2353), and conductors' dress coats with the skirt tails sewn together [64].

IV. ARTILLERY SCHOOL. [*Artilleriiskoe uchilishche.*]

9 May 1820– Unit officers, distinguished cadets, and cadets [*stroevye ofitsery, portupei-yunkery i yunkery*] of the *Artilllery School* established under the Instructional Artillery Brigade were prescribed **uniforms and arms** of the patterns for Field Foot Artillery, with the following changes:

1) Cuff flaps on the dress coat were ordered to be red, with gold galloon trim for distinguished officer candidates and officer candidates.

2) Shako plates of cadet pattern with the addition of two cannons below the eagle.

3) Unit officers were given shako plates and embroidery on the collar, cuffs, and cuff flaps, all of the patterns for Cadet Corps, but epaulettes were completely gold [65].

26 May 1820 - Unit officers, distinguished cadets, and cadets, instead of the previously prescribed two-breasted **coat**, were ordered to have single-breasted coats with red piping down the front opening and from the opening to the tails, with nine flat brass buttons (Illus. 2354 and 2355) [66].

26 January 1822– It was ordered that the shakos in the Artillery School have round **pompons**: silver for officers, and red wool for distinguished cadets and cadets (Illus. 2356) [67].

From **1824 on** – Unit officers as well as distinguished cadets and cadets began to wear a **shako** that was higher than previously, with wider cords (Illus. 2355) [68].

V. CORPS OF PAGES.[*Pazheskii korpus.*]

14 September 1802– The *Corps of Pages*, newly reorganized and taken out of the Court administration to become one of the Military Educational Institutions, was prescribed the following **uniform clothing**:
Pages– double-breasted coat of the pattern for officers, of dark-green cloth, with red collars and cuffs, gilt buttons, and gold galloon on the collar and cuffs; white pants with tall boots [*botforty*] and strap-on spurs [*nakladnye shpory*]; hats like officers', but with buttonhole loops of thin silver cord instead of galloon (Illus. 2358).
Chamber-pages[kamer-pazhi] – the same uniforms but with red piping on the skirt turnbacks and gold galloon buttonhole loops on the skirt tails. In addition to these details distinguishing them from pages, they had officers' cavalry swords [*shpagi*], without sword knots (Illus. 2358).
Pages as well as chamber-pages were prescribed long double-breasted frock coats [*syurtuki*] instead of greatcoats, lined in summer with stamin and in winter with wolf fur [*volchii mekh*].
When in formation, chamber-pages taking the places of non-commissioned officers had halberds, while pages had muskets. Both were prescribed accouterments identical to those used in Cadet Corps.
At balls at the HIGHEST Court, both chamber-pages and pages, instead of tall boots, wore white silk stockings and shoes with gilt buckles.
Officers of the Corps of Pages had the same uniforms as officers in the 1st Cadet Corps, being distinguished from them only by the tracery pattern of the embroidery on the collar, cuffs, and cuff flaps (Illus. 2359 and 2360) [69].
5 August 1807– On the **coats** of chamber-pages and pages, it was ordered to have convex instead of flat buttons, and two officers' pattern shoulder straps of the same color as the collar, trimmed around the edges with narrow gold galloon (Illus. 2361) [70].
17 September 1807– Officers of the Corps of Pages were ordered to wear **epaulettes** instead of shoulder straps, identical to those established at this time for officers of Cadet Corps (Illus. 2361) [71].
In 1812– on the **coats** of officers, chamber-pages, and pages, the high diagonally open collars were changed to low collars closed by small hooks (Illus. 2362) [72].
For **everyday use** chamber-pages and pages had dark-green double-breasted frock coats [*syurtuki*] of officers' pattern, and forage caps, and likewise wore officers' greatcoats, but of dark-green cloth instead of gray [73].

VI. GENERALS. [*Generaly.*]

Before the establishment in **1808** of a special general officer's coat, in all circumstances generals wore the uniform **coats** of those regiments and units to which they belonged.
26 January 1808– At parades, on specially tabulated holidays, and in general at any gathering of troops, generals were ordered to wear a standard newly established **general officers' coat**, of the normal pattern for officers at this time, double-breasted, of dark-green cloth, with red collar, cuffs, and turnbacks, with dark-green cuff flaps with red piping, and gold embroidery on the collar, cuffs, cuff flaps, and pocket flaps that depicted oak leaves. Gold epaulettes, white cloth pants, and tall boots [*botforty*] with spurs. With this uniform generals in the Infantry wore the normal infantry sword, those in the Heavy Cavalry—the cavalry sword, and those in the Light Cavalry—sabers. Along with this, generals were given shabracks and pistol carriers of bear fur, with St. Andrew stars (Illus. 2363 and 2364) [74].
22 January 1809– Generals serving in **garrisons** but not on the Army's list at large [*ne chislyashchies' po Armii*] were allowed to wear the standard general officer's uniform, changing only the gold embroidery, epaulettes, and buttons to silver, and to have infantry swords and—on their hat—a black plume [*sultan*] (Illus. 2365) [75].
8 June 1809 – The plumage [*plyumazh*] on generals' **hats** was removed and the previous pattern of buttonhole loop, of narrow galloon, was replaced by a new one consisting of four thick braided cords the same color as the buttons, of which the two center ones were twisted together in the form of a plait (Illus. 2365) [76].
In 1810 the high plumes used on generals' **hats** were shortened [77].

6 May 1811 – In addition to their prescribed parade coat, generals were allowed to wear the **standard army coat** described below, provided that when troops of more than one regiment were gathered at one place they were to put on the parade coat, observing this rule even in the field and when in battle against the enemy [78].

In 1812 high collars were changed to lower ones. On the parade **coat** the collar remained diagonally open as before, while on the standard army coat it was closed by means of small hooks [79].

6 April 1814 – On the embroidered **coats** of cavalry generals, instead of two rows of buttons, it was ordered that they have a single row of nine. Piping down the front opening was to be red, and both ends of the collar were to step back from the front opening for a distance of four vershoks [seven inches] (Illus. 2366). The standard army coat for cavalry generals was ordered to have the same buttons and piping, but the collar was to be closed with small hooks (Illus. 2367) [80].

In 1814 there was added to the black tape with orange checks that was on the edge of the **cockade** on general officers' hats a white tape of the same width, latter changed to silver [81].

9 September 1816 – **Garrison generals** in parade coats, instead of red collars, were ordered to have dark-green collars with red piping and the previous embroidery (Illus. 2368) [82].

7 May 1817- Generals' infantry **coats**, with embroidery as well as the standard army pattern, instead of being double-breasted, were ordered to be single-breasted, with red piping and nine buttons, following the pattern for cavalry coats. Infantry swords were to be worn with these coats, and the plume on the hat was white (Illus. 2369) [83].

24 October 1818– Generals wearing the **garrison coat** were ordered to have these single-breasted instead of double-breasted, following the pattern for infantry and cavalry coats. With this coat an infantry sword was to be worn, and the plume on the hat was white (Illus. 2370) [84].

26 June 1820 – Generals in the **Garrison Artillery** branch were ordered to have a coat of the same pattern as that prescribed for army generals, single-breasted but with a dark-green collar, and with silver embroidery, buttons, and epaulettes. An undress coat [*vitse-mundir*] was also established, identical but without embroidery [85].

7 August 1820 – Generals in the Light Cavalry were allowed to wear **moustaches** [86].

21 December 1820 – Generals assigned to the **Internal Guard** from other branches were ordered to keep the standard army coat [87].

21 May 1825 – Generals of the **Separate Lithuania Corps** and the Reserve Corps of troops under HIS IMPERIAL HIGHNESS THE TSESAREVICH CONSTANTINE PAVLOVICH were ordered to have coats, undress coats, and frock coats with raspberry collars and cuffs, with gold embroidery on parade coats (Illus. 2371 and 2372) [88].

VII. GENERAL-ADJUTANTS ANDAIDES-DE-CAMP.
[*General-Ad"yutanty i Fligel'-Ad"yutanty.*]

[Note by M.C. - General-Adjutants and Aides-de-Camp, or Flügel-Adjutants, were the special titles given to those officers in attendance on the tsar. These persons generally ceased being referred to by their rank, but rather by these titles.]

25 January 1802– With the confirmation of regulations regarding the cut, tailoring, and colors of coats for all combatant and non-combatant ranks in the Russian Army, all *General-Adjutants in the Infantry* were prescribed a coat of the standard officer's pattern, with two rows of buttons, of dark-green cloth, red collar, cuffs, skirt tail lining, and turnbacks; dark-green cuff flaps; gold embroidery on the collar and cuff flaps, gold buttons and aiguilette; white pants; hat with white plumage around the edge and a black plume; gloves without cuffs; infantry sword (Illus. 2373). *General-Adjutants in the Cavalry* were prescribed the exact same coat as in the Infantry, but white instead of dark green, with a cavalry sword and white plume.

Infantry Aides-de-Camp were prescribed uniforms as for infantry General-Adjutants, and *cavalry aides-de-camp*—as for cavalry General-Adjutants, with only gold changed to silver and without plumage on the hat (Illus. 2374). All General-Adjutants and Aides-de-Camp retained their previous sashes and canes, but were given dark-green shabracks and pistol carriers with galloon the same color as the buttons [89].

17 September 1807 – General-Adjutants and Aides-de-Camp were ordered to wear, on the left shoulder, an **epaulette** the same color as the buttons and corresponding to the rank of the wearer by means of the same patterns established at this time for Guards troops, and along with this keeping the aiguillette on the right shoulder (Illus. 2375) [90].

12 November 1808– **Cavalry** General-Adjutants and Aides-de-Camp were allowed to wear an **undress coat** of the same pattern as the white coat, but in dark green and worn with likewise dark-green **pants**. Infantry General-Adjutants and Aides-de-Camp, on the other hand, were allowed when off duty to have dark-green pants instead of white. From this year, all General-Adjutants and Aides-de-Camp were allowed to wear **frock coats** of dark-green cloth, with a red collar and cuffs, and with buttons the same color as those on the dress coats [91].

Since 1812 the high collars on the **coats** of General-Adjutants and Aides-de-Camp were replaced by low collars closed with small hooks [92].

30 August 1815 and **26 January 1816** – General-Adjutants and Aides-de-Camp in the **cavalry** were ordered to have single-breasted **coats** instead of double-breasted, with nine buttons and white piping down the front opening, as well as on the collar, cuffs, cuff flaps, pocket flaps, skirt turnbacks, and pocket folds [skladki karmanov]. The previous red cuffs were replaced by dark green, and the dark-green cuff flaps—by red. Apart from the embroidery that retained its existing tracery pattern, an embroidered edge was added to the collar, cuffs, and cuff flaps. Instead of one epaulette it was ordered to have two, with the HIGHEST monogram under an IMPERIAL crown, in silver for General-Adjutants and in gold for Aides-de-Camp. Officers of Light Cavalry holding these appointments were prescribed, instead of high *botfory* boots, hussar boots and sabers (Illus. 2376, 2377, 2378, and 2379). The changes in uniforms noted here also applied to General-Adjutants and Aides-de-Camp in the infantry, but with the difference that they kept the previous double-breasted coat and did not have white piping down the front or from the front opening to the skirt tails [93]. Shabracks and pistol carriers (for Infantry and Heavy Cavalry) and saddlecloths (for Light Cavalry) were prescribed to be of white cloth with red trim, with galloon and stars: gold for General-Adjutants and silver for Aides-de-Camps [94].

7 May 1817 – **Infantry** General-Adjutants and Aides-de-Camp were ordered to have, instead of a double-breasted **coat**, a single-breasted one similar in all respects to the pattern established in 1815 for cavalry General-Adjutants and Aides-de-Camp [95].

VIII. AT LARGE IN THE ARMY, CAVALRY, AND ARTILLERY.
[*Sostoyashchie po armii, kavalerii i artillerii.*]

25 January 1802– *Field and company-grade officers at large in the Army and Cavalry* were given the same **uniforms** as established at this time for General-Adjutants: in the Army—as for infantry General-Adjutants (Illus. 2380), and in the Cavalry—as for cavalry General-Adjutants, but without embroidery and aiguilettes and without plumage around the hat [96].

17 September 1807– These same personnel were given **epaulettes** on both shoulders, of the pattern established at this same time for officers of Grenadier regiments, except completely gold in color (Ilus. 2381) [97].

In 1808 officers at large in the Army, when not on duty, were allowed to wear dark-green cloth **pants** instead of white, while such officers in the Cavalry, also when not on duty, were allowed dark-green coats and pants. Both groups of officers were permitted to wear dark-green **frock coats** with red collars and cuffs [98].

From 1812 unattached officers in the Army and Cavalry began to wear **collars** on dress coats and frock coats without the front diagonal opening, lower than before and closed by small hooks (Illus. 2382) [99].

26 June 1820 – Field and company-grade officers at large in the **Field Foot Artillery** were ordered to wear, with their Artillery coat, epaulettes that were all gold [100].

IX. STAFF DUTY OFFICERS, SENIOR ADJUTANTS, and ADJUTANTS to GENERAL OFFICERS.
[*Dezhurnye shtab-ofitser i starshie i general'skie ad"yutanty.*]

16 July 1806– Guards officers acting as adjutants to general officers were ordered to wear the **uniform** of the regiment in which they served before being appointed as adjutants. These same adjutants coming from Army officers were prescribed the standard army uniform, for infantry or cavalry in accordance with the officer's combat arm, but with a gold aiguilette. Artillery and engineer adjutants were ordered to wear the uniforms of their corps, but with aiguilettes the same color as their buttons [101].

17 September 1807 – These officers were given **epaulettes** of the same color as their buttons, of the pattern established at this time for regiments of Army and Guards Infantry and Cavalry [102].

From 1812the high **collars** were replaced by lower ones closed with small hooks [103].

30 August 1815 and **26 January 1816** – Senior adjutants and general officers' adjutants, at large in the **Army Heavy and Light Cavalry**, were prescribed uniforms exactly like those established at this time for cavalry Aides-de-Camp, except with embroidery replaced by buttonhole loops (Illus. 2383, 2384, and 2385). Those adjutants at large in the **Infantry** were prescribed uniforms as for infantry Aides-de-Camp, with the same embroidery as for cavalry Adjutants (infantry as well as cavalry) who were on the rolls of Guards regiments, and regardless of buttonholes loops, they were ordered to also have on the collar, cuffs, and cuff flaps an embroidered silver edge (Illus. 2383, 2385, and 2386) [104], and the same shabracks, pistol carriers, and saddlecloths as established at this time for Aides-de-Camp, i.e. white with red trim and silver galloon: for Guards—with silver St. Andrew stars, and for the Army—without stars [105]. Staff duty officers were ordered to have uniforms as for general officers' adjutants, but without an aiguillette and with the same shabracks and saddlecloths as Adjutants (Illus. 2387) [106].

25 October 1816 – Adjutants from the **Separate Corps of the Internal Guard** were ordered to have the same uniforms as prescribed for Army Infantry adjutants assigned to general officers, but with the red collar replaced by dark green (Illus. 2388) [107].

7 May 1817– All Staff Duty Officers as well as senior adjutants and general officers' adjutants from the infantry were ordered to have **coats** of the pattern for cavalry adjutants, i.e. single-breasted instead of double-breasted, with nine buttons in front and white piping down the front opening and from there to the skirt tails (Illus. 2389 and 2390) [108].

26 June 1820 – Adjutants to **Garrison** generals and district chiefs of Artillery garrisons were ordered to have a coat identical to that prescribed for generals' adjutants in the Corps of the Internal Guard [109].

21 May 1825– The Staff Duty Officer and all adjutants in the **Separate Lithuania Corps** and Reserve Corps of forces under the command of HIS IMPERIAL HIGHNESS THE TSESAREVICH CONSTANTINE PAVLOVICH were ordered to have raspberry cloth piping, instead of red, on their coats and frocks (Illus. 2391) [110].

X. TOWN MAJORS, GATE MAJORS, TOWN ADJUTANTS, and BUILDINGS ADJUTANTS. [*Plats-Maiory, Maiory ot-Vorot i Plats i Bau-Ad"yutanty.*]

23 August 1824– All Town Majors and Town Adjutants were ordered to have a **uniform** identical to that prescribed for senior adjutants and general officers' adjutants, with only the replacement of red cloth by orange and without aiguilettes (Ilus. 2392) [111].

28 January 1825 – The exact same **uniform** was prescribed for all Buildings Adjutants and Gate Majors. These, as well as Town Majors and Town Adjutants, if they were in Guards regiments, were ordered to have on their coat's collar, cuffs, and cuff flaps, in addition to buttonhole loops, a silver edging, while those in the Light cavalry were to wear hussar boots and cavalry sabers. The latter were also given shabracks, pistol carriers, and saddlecloths identical to those for adjutants, of white cloth but with orange between the galloon instead of red, and for those in also in the guard—with St.-Andrew stars (Illus. 2393) [112].

21 April 1825– All Town Majors, Town Adjutants, Buildings Adjutants, and Gate Majors, when in the course of their duties obliged to command guard mounts, were ordered to not wear their **hats** fore-and-aft [*s polya*], but rather athwart [*po forme*] [113].

XI. WAGONMASTERS AND PROVOSTS. [*Wagenmeistery i Geval'digery.*]

25 January 1816– The *Wagonmaster-General [General-Wagenmeister]*, if he held general officer rank, was ordered to have a uniform similar to that for cavalry generals' adjutants, with the coat's red collar and cuff flaps replaced by blue [*svetlos-inii*], and with silver general officers' embroidery and edging (Illus. 2394). The *Provost-General [General-Geval'diger]* was prescribed the same **uniform** as the Wagonmaster-General, but double-breasted instead of single-breasted and without white piping down the front opening, following the pattern for infantry coats (Illus. 2395). These same persons, if they did not hold general officer rank, were authorized to have the prescribed embroidery only on the front of the collar. A *Senior Wagonmaster [Ober-Vagenmeister]* and *Divisional Wagonmaster [Divizionyi Vagenmeister]*, as well as a *Senior Provost*and

Divisional Provost, were prescribed the same uniforms as the preceding ranks but without guards embroidery, instead of which they were ordered to have buttonhole lace; those in Army regiments—without any silver edging, while those in Guards regiments—with edging on the collar, cuffs, and cuff flaps (Illus. 2396 and 2397) [114].

18 February 1820 – Brigade commanders of **Train battalions** who were at the same time Corps Wagonmasters were ordered to wear the Senior Wagonmaster uniform, while battalion commanders who at the same time were appointed as Divisional Wagonmasters were directed to wear the uniform prescribed for officers of Train battalions [115].

XII. RETIRED PERSONNEL. [*Otstavnye.*]

14 March 1802– Retired officers who had served on active military service without reproach for twenty years were permitted to wear the **uniform** of the regiment or position to which they belonged when they were granted retirement, even though they had not served for ten years in commissioned officer rank [116].

22 November 1802– The aforementioned privilege was extended to knights of the military order of **St. George** who had taken retirement, regardless of the amount of time they had been in military service [117].

17 February 1816– **Adjutants** released from service upon their own request and with the right to wear the uniform were ordered to wear the uniforms of those regiments to which they last belonged during their service [118].

12 November 1817 – Generals and field and company-grade officers released from service with the right to wear the uniform were ordered not to wear **epaulettes** [119].

XIII. ORDERLIES. [*Den'shchiki.*]

17 March 1802– For everyday use orderlies were prescribed the following **uniform** clothing: cloth caftan or coat, single-breasted (in the Life-Guards Horse Regiment—very dark blue, in Dragoon and Jäger regiments—light green, in all other units—dark green), with lining and trim on the skirt and tails the same color as the coat; with a falling collar and round cuffs of the color prescribed for the coat of the person on whom the orderly attends; with covered cloth buttons, of which 8 were prescribed to be on the right side of the front opening, 2 at the waist, and 3 on the cuffs along the lower hem of the sleeve; instead of a neckcloth a black handkerchief; a greatcoat indentical to those of the soldiers of the regiment whose officer the orderly attends, but without shoulder straps; pants and boots the same as for the person on whom the orderly attends; officer pattern hat, with button and buttonhole loop of narrow galloon the same color as the regiment's buttons. In Guards regiments for the orderlies of generals and field and company-grade officers, but in Army regiments only for the orderlies of generals and field-grade officers, the brim of the hat was trimmed with wide galloon, without crenellation, the same color as the buttons. In addtion, orderlies in all Guards forces had a ribbon or cockade of black tape on the hat (Illus. 2398) [120].

17 May 1819 – Orderlies were ordered to have **greatcoats** with long falling collars [short capes – M.C.] as for officers, but trimmed around the edges with cloth stripes: in the Guards—three rows, and in the Army—two. The width of these stripes as well as the distance between them was defined to be one half vershok [7/8 inch]. The color of the stripe and of the smaller, standing, collar was prescribed to be the same as the collar on the dress coat of that general or field or company-grade officer whom the orderly served. **Forage caps** were also given to orderlies, of the same pattern as for soldiers but with a visor of dark-green cloth, with a band the same color as the greatcoat's standing collar (except for the Life-Guards Izmailovskii and Pavlovskii Regiments, where the band was white), and red piping along the top and sides of the crown (Illus. 2399) [121].

XIV. FLAGS and STANDARDS of REGULAR FORCES.
[*Znamena i shtandarty regulyarnykh voisk.*]

Upon EMPEROR ALEXANDER I's ascension to the throne, each Fusilier company in the Guards and Grenadier regiments and each Musketeer company in Musketeer and Garrison regiments had one standard [*sic*, flag – M.C.]. In each Infantry, Grenadier, Musketeer, and Garrison regiment one flag, and in each Guards and Army Cavalry regiment one standard, was white, and the remaining flags and standards colored. Flags were not authorized for Jäger, Artillery, and Pioneer regiments. *Poles* kept the same colors (straw-colored, black, white, and coffee-colored in the Infantry, and green in the Cavalry) as they had during the preceding reign. Subsequently, from 1801 through 1825, there were the following changes in the numbers of flags and standards, and in the colors of flag poles:

a) *In the numbers of flags and standards.*

21 March 1802– Regiments of Guards Infantry, and also of Grenadiers, Musketeers, and Garrisons, were ordered to keep only two flags in each battalion: in first battalions one was white and the other colored, and in the other battalions all were colored [122].

In 1813, while the forces were outside the country, Foot regiments in the Life-Guards and Grenadier regiments were ordered to keep only one colored flag in each battalion [123].

31 August 1814– The preceding order was extended to Infantry (formerly called Musketeer) regiments [124].

4 November 1814 – All Cavalry regiments were ordered to have only three colored standards each, with one authorized for each division [*diviziya*, i.e. double-squadron], and thus white flags as well as white standards were completed eliminated [125].

25 June 1821– The regulations for flags, from 1813 and 31 August 1814 and set forth above, were extended to Garrison regiments and battalions [126]. Internal Garrison battalions, which from 1811 formed the Corps of the Internal Guard, were not authorized any flags.

b) *In the colors for flag poles.*

5 December 1808 – Flag poles were ordered to have the following colors: *in the first* Grenadier and Musketeer regiments of divisions—yellow, *in the second*—black, *in the third*—white, *in the fourth*—yellow, *in the fifth*—black, and in all Garrisons—coffee-colored. The length of the pole was set at 5 arshins [140 inches] [127].

17 July 1816 – It was ordered that *the first* regiments of Grenadier and Infantry divisions have yellow flag poles, *the second*—black, *the third*—white, and *the fourth*—coffee-colored [128].

23 January 1819 – It was ordered that *the first* regiments of Guards, Infantry, Grenadier, and Infantry divisions have straw-colored flag poles, *the second*—black, *the third*—white, and *the fourth*—coffee-colored. In the Guards Équipage and all Carabinier and Jäger regiments the poles were to be black. In the L.-Gds. Sapper Battalion the pole was of lacquered mountain ash [*ryabinovago dereva, pod lakom*], and in Army Sapper and Pioneer battalions—yellow [129]. (Note: Lists of regiments, from which it may be seen what number a regiment occupied within a division, are located in Volume X of this work. Flags were granted to Carabinier and Jäger regiments only in cases of a special distinction.)

a) *Grenadier and Musketeer (from 1811 renamed Infantry) regiments.*

In 1803 seven drawings were confirmed for the flags of Musketeer regiments (that would henceforth be conferred): 1) black cross, red corners; 2) sky-blue cross, white corners; 3) green cross, white corners; 4) yellow cross, white corners; 5) raspberry cross, white corners; 6) dark-blue cross, white cross; 7) orange cross, white corners. On each flag, within an orange circle enclosed by two gold branches tied by a gold ribbon, was the image of a two-headed eagle with one raised and one lowered wing, and gold crowns, beaks, and thunder bolts. Over the circle and between the tips of the branches was an IMPERIAL crown, and in the corners—IMPERIAL monograms and gold branches and crowns. *For white flags*, with the same depiction, the cross and corners were white (Illus. 2400, 2401, and 2402) [130]. Flags as specified by these drawings were granted to the following regiments:

A) *1 white and 5 with a black cross and red corners* (Illus. 2400 and 2401, a):

In 1803 – to the *Petrovsk* Musketeer Regiment.

B) *1 white and 5 with a sky-blue [goluboi] cross and white corners* (Illus. 2400 and 2401, b):

In 1803 – to the *Kopore* Musketeer Regiment.

In 1805 – to the *Kaluga* Musketeer Regiment.

C) *1 white and 5 with a green cross and white corners* (Illus. 2400 and 2401, c):

In 1805 – to the *Volhynia* Musketeer Regiment.

In 1805 – to the *Mogilev* Musketeer Regiment.

In 1805 – to the *Kostroma* Musketeer Regiment.

In 1805 – to the *Yakutsk* Musketeer Regiment.

In 1805 – to the *Nyslott* Musketeer Regiment.

In 1805 – to the *Okhotsk* Musketeer Regiment.

In 1805 – to the *Pernau* Musketeer Regiment.

In 1814 – to the *Mogilev* Infantry Regiment.

D) *1 white and 5 with a yellow cross and white corners* (Illus. 2400 and 2401, d):

In 1803 – to the *Tobolsk* Musketeer Regiment.

In 1805 – to the *Vilna* Musketeer Regiment.

In 1805 – to the *Penza* Musketeer Regiment.

E) *1 white and 5 with a raspberry [malinovyi] cross and white corners* (Illus. 2400 and 2402, a):

In 1803 – to the *Galich* Musketeer Regiment.

In 1805 – to the *Estonia* Musketeer Regiment.

In 1812 – to the *Troitsk* Infantry Regiment.

F) *1 white and 5 with a dark-blue cross and white corners* (Illus. 2400 and 2402, b):

In 1803 – to the *Crimea* Musketeer Regiment.

In 1803 – to the *Vologda* Musketeer Regiment.

In 1803 – to the *1st, 2nd, 3rd,* and *4th* Marine Regiments.

In 1805 – to the *Odessa* Musketeer Regiment.

In 1807 – to the *Libau* Musketeer Regiment.

In 1807 – to the *Kamchatka* Musketeer Regiment.

In 1807 – to the *Mingrelia* Musketeer Regiment.

G) *1 white and 1 with a dark-blue cross and white corners* (Illus. 2400 and 2402, b):

In 1805 – to the *Caspian* Marine Battalion.

In 1811 – to the *1st* and *2nd Instructional* Grenadier Battalions.

H) *1 white and 5 with an orange cross and white corners* (Illus. 2400 and 2402, c):

In 1803 – to the *Kura* Musketeer Regiment.

In subsequent years flags of the same pattern but with changes in the colors were granted to these regiments:

In 1804 – To the *Moscow* Grenadiers—1 white flag and 5 with a black cross and red corners with inscriptions in gold Cyrillic letters on sky-blue ribbons over the eagle: "*S nami Bog*; and under the eagle: "*Za vzyatie znamya u Frantsuzov pri rekakh Trebii in Nure, 1799*" ["*God with us*" and "*For taking a flag from the French at the Trebbia and Nure rivers, 1799*"] (Illus. 2403, a).

In 1807 – To the *Kiev* Grenadiers—1 white and 5 with a rose cross, white corners, and the inscription (in gold Cyrillic letters) on outer edges of the cross: "*Za podvig pri Shengraben, 4-go Noyabrya 1805 goda v srazhenii 5 t korpusa s nepriyatelem, sostoyavshim iz 30 t*" ["*For the feat at Schöngraben, 4 November 1805 in a combat of a 5-thousand strong corps with 30 thousand enemy*"]. For this flag's spearhead, instead of a gold two-headed eagle, there was a gold finial in the form of a St.-George cross, and instead of the tassels hanging from silver ribbon, they were on the colored ribbon of that knightly order (Illus. 2403 b). This was the first example of Russian Army troops being awarded the flag that would subsequently be called the *St.-George flag [Georgievskoe znamya]*.

In 1807 – The *Villmanstrand, Brest, Kremenchug,* and *Minsk* Musketeers—each 1 white and 5 with a gray [*dikii*] cross and white corners (Illus. 2403 c).

In 1808 – To the *Bialystok* Musketeers—1 white flag and a 5 with dark-blue cross and red corners (Illus. 2403 d).

In 1809 – To the *Pernau* Musketeers—St.-George flags: 1 white and 5 with a green cross and white corners, all with the inscription "*Za vzyatie u Frantsuzov dvukh znamen v srazhenii pri Geil'sberg 29 Maya i pri Fridlande 2-go iyunya 1807 goda*" ["*For capturing two flags from the French in battle at Heilsberg 29 May and Friedland 2 June 1807*"] (Illus. 2403 a).

In 1809 – To the *Schlüsselburg* Musketeers—St.-George flags: 1 white and 5 with a rose-colored cross and green corners, all with the inscription "*Za vzyatie u Frantsuzov 2-go Iyunya 1807 goda pod gorodom Fridlandom odnogo znamya*" ["*For capturing a flag from the French on 2 June 1807 at the town of Friedland*"] (Illus. 2404 b).

In 1809 – To the *Azov* Musketeers—1 white and 5 with an orange cross and black corners (Illus. 2404 c).

In 1809 – To the *Phanagoria* Grenadiers—6 St.-George flags: of the same colors as for the Schlüsselburg Regiment, with the inscription "*Za vzyatie pristupom Bazardzhika 22 Maya 1810 goda*" ["*For the capture by assault of Bazardzhik 22 May 1810*"] (Illus. 2404 d).

In 1810 – To the *Narva* Musketeers—5 flags with an orange cross and sky-blue corners (Illus. 2405 a).

In 1810 – To the *Dnieper* Musketeers—a flag with a yellow cross and corners half white and half black (Illus. 2405 b).

In 1812 – To the *Georgia* Grenadiers—St.-George flags: 1 white and 5 with a dark-blue cross and yellow corners, all with the inscription "*Za otlichnuyu khrabrost' pri vzyatii shturmom turetskoi kreposti Akhalkalaka s 7 na 8-e chislo Dekabrya 1811 goda*" ["*For distinguished courage in the storming of the Turkish fortress of Akhalkalaka from 7 to 8 December 1811*"] (Illus. 2405 c).

In 1812 – To the *Odessa* Infantry—1 white and 5 with a yellow cross and corners half white and half black, identical to those granted to the Dnieper Musketeer Regiment in 1810.

In 1812 – To the *Vilna* Infantry—1 white and 5 with a white cross and red corners (Illus. 2405 d).

In 1812 – To the *Tarnopol* Infantry—1 white and 5 with a yellow cross and red corners (Illus. 2406 a).

In 1812 – To the *Simbirsk* Infantry—1 white and 5 with a green cross and red corners (Illus. 2406 b).

In 1814 – To the *Perm* Infantry—1 white and 5 with a light-brown [*svetlo-korichnevyi*] cross and green corners (Illus. 2406 c).

In 1814 – To *Graf Arkacheev's Grenadiers* and the *Chernigov* and *Sevsk* Infantry—St.-George flags: each 1 white and 5 with a green cross and white corners, identical to those granted to the Pernau Regiment in 1809, but with the inscription *"Za otlichie pri porazhenii i izgnanii nepriyatelya iz predelov Rossii 1812 goda"* [*"For distinction in the defeat and expulsion of the enemy from Russian territory in 1812"*]. To the *Okhotsk* and *Kamchatka* Infantry—the same flags with the inscription *"Za otlichnoe muzhestvo i muzhestvo i khrabrost' v voine s Frantsieyu 1812, 1813 i 1814 godov"* [*"For distinguished courage and bravery in the war with France in 1812, 1813, and 1814"*], and to the *Ryazsk* Infantry—the same flags with the inscription *"Za vozdayanie otlichnykh podvigov, okazannykh v blagopoluchno-okonchennuyu kampaniyu 1814 goda"* [*"For performing distinguished deeds during the successfully concluded campaign of 1814"*].

In 1815 – To the *Orel* Infantry—three St.-George flags with the inscription: *"V vozdayanie otlichnykh podvigov, okazannykh v srazheniyakh 1814 goda: Yanvarya 17-go dnya pri Brienn-Leshato i 20-go pri selenii La-Rotier"* [*"For distinguished feats during the 1814 battles: at Brienne-le-Châteauon 17 January and the village of La Rothièreon the 20th"*]. Except for the inscription, these were identical to the colored flags for the preceding regiments.

19 July 1816 – HIGHEST Confirmation was given to new drawings of flags for Grenadier and Infantry regiments, different from the previous patterns in that they depicted a two-headed eagle with both wings lowered and on its breast the Moscow coat-of-arms (St. George on a horse, on a red field). For all regiments the cross was prescribed to be green while the corners were by regiment:

A) *In regiments of the 1st Grenadier Division* – upper half red, lower white (Illus. 2407 a).

B) *In regiments of the 2nd Grenadier Division* – upper half red, lower black (Illus. 2407 b).

C) *In regiments of the 3rd Grenadier Division* – upper half red, lower yellow (Illus. 2407 c).

D) *In regiments of infantry divisions* – white corners (Illus. 2407 d).

Flags in accordance with these drawings were granted to the following regiments:

1st Grenadier Division:

In 1816 – To the *Emperor of Austria's* and the *King of Prussia's* regiments—plain flags without inscriptions.

2nd Grenadier Division:

In 1824 – To the *Kiev* Regiment—St.-George flags, with the inscription: *"Za podvig pri Shengraben 4-go Noyabrya 1805 goda, v srazhenii 5 t. korpusa s nepriyatelem, sostoyavshim iz 30 t."* [*"For the feat at Schöngraben, 4 November 1805 in a combat of a 5-thousand strong corps with 30 thousand enemy"*]; to the *Taurica* Regiment—St.-George flags with the inscription: *"Za vzyatie znameni v srazhenii protiv Frantsuzov v Gollandii pod gorodom Bergen v 1799 godu"* [*"For capturing a flag in battle against the French in Holland at the town of Bergen in 1799"*]; to the *Yekaterinoslav* Regiment— plain flags without on inscription; to the *Moscow* Regiment—St-George flags with the inscription: *"Za vzyatie znameni u Frantsuzov pri Trebia in Nure 1799 goda"* [*"For capturing a flag from the French at the Trebbia and Nure in 1799"*].

3rd Grenadier Division:

In 1824 – To the *Siberia, Little Russia,* and *Astrakhan* Regiments—plain, without inscriptions; to the *Phanagoria* Regiment—St.-George flags with the inscription: *"Za vzyatie pristupom Bazardzhika 22-go Maya 1810 goda"* [*"For the taking of Bazardzhik by storm 22 May 1810"*].

Marine regiments:

In 1818 – To the 1st, 2nd, 3rd, and 4th Regiments, plain, without inscriptions.

Infantry regiments:

In 1816 – To the *Orel* Regiment—plain, without an inscription, and to the *Butyrskii*—St.-George flags, with the inscription: *"Za srazhenie 23-go Fevralya 1814 goda bliz mestechka Krazha"* [*"For the fight near the hamlet of Grange 23 February 1814"*].

In 1817 – To the *Borodino* and *Tarutino* Regiments—plain, without inscriptions.

In 1818 – To *Prince William of Prussia's,* the *Velikie-Luki, Vologda, Galich, Saratov,* and *Voronezh* Regiments—plain, without inscriptions.

In 1819 – To the *Pskov* and *New Ingermanland* Regiments—plain, without inscriptions.

In 1822 – To the *Smolensk* Regiment—St.-George flags with the inscription: *"Za vzyatie Frantsuzskikh znamen na gorakh*

Al'piiskikh" ["For the capture of French flags in the Alps"]; to the Vladimir, Suzdal, Uglich, and Yaroslav Regiments—plain, without inscriptions.

In 1823 – To the Murom Regiment-- plain, without inscriptions.

In 1824 – To Prince Charles of Prussia's, the Reval, Old Ingermanland, Belozersk, Olonets, Ladoga, Kostroma, Nizhnii-Novgorod, Nizovsk, Simbirsk, Troitsk, Penza, Vitebsk, Poltava, Aleksopol, Yelets, Bryansk, Kursk, Staryi-Oskol, Rylsk, Moscow, Ryazan, Belev, and Tula Regiments-- plain, without inscriptions; to the Schlüsselburg Regiment—St.-George flags with the inscription: "2-go iyunya 1807 goda, za vzyatie pod Fridland odnogo znamya u Frantsuzov" ["2 June 1807, for the capture of a flag from the French at Friedland"].

In 1818 two flags each were presented to the newly formed 1st and 2nd (from 1825 Samogitia and Lutsk) Grenadier Regiments, identical with those established in 1816 for regiments of the 1st Grenadier Division, but with the Lithuania coat-of-arms on the breast of the eagle instead of Moscow's, i.e. instead of St. George the Bearer of Victory. [Note: A depiction of the Lithuania coat-of-arms, i.e. a galloping Lithuanian horseman, is shown below, on the drawings for the L.-Gds. Lithuania and L.-Gds. Volhynia Regiments.]

b) Army Cavalry regiments.

In 1803 – drawings were confirmed for cavalry standards: white with gold corners and green with white corners (in the form of oval shields), on which the IMPERIAL monogram is embroidered between two laurel wreaths, under a crown. In the middle of the standard's field is a two-headed eagle with one raised and one lowered wing, and in the upper corner, facing the upraised wing—rays of light. All this decoration, and in general all embroidery and fringe, was gold (Illus. 2408). Standards of this pattern (1 white and 4 green, i.e. one for each squadron) were granted to the following Army Cavalry regiments:

In 1804 – To the Courland, Pereyaslavl, Borisoglebsk, and New Russia Dragoons.

In 1805 – To the Livland and Zhitomir Dragoons.

In 1809 – To the Tiraspol, Dorpat, Nezhin, Yamburg, Serpukhov, and Arzamas Dragoons.

In 1812 – To the Astrakhan and Novgorod Cuirassiers.

The same standards, except with certain changes, were granted to the following regiments:

In 1807 – To the Chernigov Dragoons (1 white and 4 green) and the Pavlograd Hussars (1 white and 9 green); St.-George standards, with the inscription "Za podvig pri Shengraben, 4 Noyabrya 1805, v srazhenii 5 t. korpusa s nepriyatelem, sostayavshim iz 30 t." ["For the feat at Schöngraben, 4 November 1805 in a combat of a 5-thousand strong corps with 30 thousand enemy"] (Illus. 2409a).

In 1807 – To the Mitau and Finland Dragoons (each 1 white and 4 green), with the addition of a gold cross in the upper corner under the light rays (Illus. 2409b).

In 1808 – To the St. Petersburg Dragoons (1 white and 4 green); St.-George standards with the inscription: "Za vzyatie u Frantsuzov trekh znamen v srazheniyakh: 1805 goda Noyabrya 8 pri derevne Gauzet i 1807 Yanvarya 26 i 27 pod gorodom Fridlandom" ["For taking three flags from the French at the battles at the village of Gauzet on 8 November 1805 and the town of Friedland on 26 and 27 January 1807"]. In addition to the inscriptions, these were identical to the St.-George standards awarded in 1807 to the Chernigov and Pavlograd regiments.

In 1810 – To the Starodub Dragoons (1 white and 4 green); St.-George standards with the inscription: "Za vzyatie pristupom Bazardzhika 22-go Maya 1810 goda" ["For the taking of Bazardzhik by storm 22 May 1810"]. Except for the inscription, these were identical to the preceding standards.

In 1814 – To the Yekaterinoslav, Glukhov, and Little Russia Cuirassiers (each 1 white and 5 green, i.e. one for each operational squadron), with the inscription: "Za otlichie pri porazhenii i izgnanii nepriyatelya iz predelov Rossii 1812 goda" ["For distinction in the defeat and expulsion of the enemy from Russian territory in 1812"]. Except for the inscription, these were identical to the preceding standards.

In 1815 – To the Kiev and Kharkov Dragoons (3 green standards each, i.e. one for each double-squadron [division]), St.-George pattern identical to the preceding but with the inscription: "Za otlichie protiv nepriyatelya v srazhenii u Katsbakha 14 Avgusta 1813 goda" ["For distinction against the enemy in the battle of Katzbach 14 August 1813". To the New Russia Dragoons and the Sumy Hussars—the same, and in the same numbers, with the inscription "V vozdayanie otlichnykh podvigov, okazannykh v blagopoluchno-okonchennuyu kampaniyu 1814 goda" ["In recognition of distinguished deeds performed in the victorious 1814 campaign"]

In 1816 – To the *Izyum* Hussars—St.-George standards identical to those for the four preceding regiments, and in the same number, with the inscription: *"Za otlichie pri porazhenii i izgnanii nepriyatelya iz predelov Rossii 1812 goda"* [*"For distinction in the defeat and expulsion of the enemy from Russian territory in 1812"*].

c) *Garrison regiments and battalions.*

Garrison regiments and battalions were authorized the same flags as established in 1803 for Grenadier and Musketeer regiments, except without monograms in the corners. One flag for each regiment or separate battalion was white, and the rest were colored with white corners. During the reign of EMPEROR ALEXANDER I flags of this pattern were granted as follows:

A) For each unit, 1 white flag and 3 with a green cross (Illus. 2410a):

In 1805 – To the *Vilna, Minsk,* and *Grodno* battalions.

B) 1 white flag and 3 with a raspberry cross (Illus. 2410b):

In 1805 – To the *Yekaterinoslav* battalion.

C) For each unit, 1 white flag and 3 with a dark-blue cross (Illus. 2410c):

In 1805 – To the *Vladikavkaz* and *Kamenets-Podolia* battalions.

D) For each unit, 1 white flag and 3 with an orange cross (Illus. 2411a):

In 1805 – To the *Vologda* and *Velikii-Ustyug* battalions.

In 1807 – To the *Penza* battalion.

E) For each unit, 1 white flag and 3 with a coffee-colored cross (Illus. 2411b):

In 1808 – To the *Ufa* and *Vyatka* battalions.

F) 1 white flag and 3 with a green cross and gold corners with the IMPERIAL monogram (Illus. 2411c):

In 1810 – To the *Sveaborg* Garrison Regiment. (*Note:* Of all these garrisons, during the reign of EMPEROR ALEXANDER I only the Sveaborg regiment was given flags with monograms in the corners.)

d) *Guards Infantry units.*

In 1811 – The newly formed *Life-Guards Lithuania Regiment* was granted flags of the pattern used at that time by Army Infantry regiments, in the following colors: for one flag—a white cross and corners that were half straw-colored and half black, and for five flags—a straw-colored cross and corners that were half white and half black (Illus. 2412).

In 1813 – The following Life-Guards regiments that had distinguished themselves in military actions were authorized St.-George flags similar to the preceding ones for the L.-Gds. Lithuania Regiment, but with the following differences in colors and inscriptions:

For the *L.-Gds. Preobrazhenskii Regiment*: 1 with a white cross and corners, and 5 with a yellow cross and red corners; inscription: *"Za okazannye podvigi v srazhenii 17 Avgusta 1813 goda pri Teplits"* [*"For deeds performed at the battle of Teplitz 17 August 1813"*] (Illus. 2412a).

For the *L.-Gds. Semenovskii Regiment*: the same as above, and in the same numbers, but blue [*svetlosinii*] corners on the colored flags (Illus. 2412b).

For the *L.-Gds. Izmailovskii Regiment*: the same as above, and in the same numbers, but white corners on the colored flags, and all with the inscription: *"Za otlichie pri porazhenii i izgnanii nepriyatelya iz predelov Rossii 1812 goda"* [*"For distinction in the defeat and expulsion of the enemy from Russian territory in 1812"*] (Illus. 2412c).

For the *L.-Gds. Jäger Regiment*: the same as above, and in the same numbers, but the colored flags with corners half black and half green (Illus. 2412d).

For the *L.-Gds. Lithuania Regiment*: 1 with a white cross and yellow and green corners; 5 with a yellow cross and corners that were half white and half green; the same inscription as the preceding (Illus. 2413a and 2413b).

For the *L.-Gds. Grenadier Regiment*: the same as for the Izmailovskii and Jägers, and in the same numbers, but with blue corners on the colored flags (Illus. 2413c).

For the *L.-Gds. Pavlovsk Regiment*: the same, and in the same numbers, but the colored flags with corners half blue and half white (Illus. 2414a).

For the *L.-Gds. Finland Regiment*: the same, and in the same numbers, but with green corners on the colored flags (Illus. 2414b).

In place of these flags, which were not delivered to the regiments, three flags were granted to each regiment, of the pattern confirmed in 1816 for Grenadier and Infantry regiments, but in different colors, namely: yellow cross, with corners and inscriptions varying by regiment.

In 1814 – To the *L.-Gds. Preobrazhenskii Regiment*: upper half of the corners—red, lower half—white; inscription "*Za okazannye podvigi v srazhenii 17 Avgusta 1813 goda, pri Kul'm*" [*"For feets demonstrated on 17 August 1813 and the Battle of Kulm"*] (Illus. 2415a).

In the same year, to the *L.-Gds. Semenovskii Regiment*: upper half of corners blue, lower white; the same inscription as the preceding (Illus. 2415b).

In the same year, to the *L.-Gds. Izmailovskii Regiment*: the entire corner—white; inscription "*Za otlichie pri porazhenii i izgnanii nepriyatelya iz predelov Rossii 1812 goda*" [*"For distinction in the defeat and expulsion of the enemy from Russian territory in 1812"*] (Illus. 2415c).

In the same year, to the *L.-Gds. Jäger Regiment*: upper half of corners green, lower white; the same inscription as for the L.-Gds. Izmailovskii Regiment (Illus. 2415d).

In 1817 – To the *L.-Gds. Moscow Regiment* (the former L.-Gds. Lithuania Regiment): upper half red, lower black; the same inscription as for the L.-Gds. Izmailovskii Regiment (Illus. 2416a).

In the same year, to the *L.-Gds. Grenadier Regiment*: upper half blue, lower black; the same inscription as for the L.-Gds. Izmailovskii Regiment (Illus. 2416b).

In the same year, to the *L.-Gds. Pavlovsk Regiment*: upper half white, lower black; the same inscription as for the L.-Gds. Izmailovskii Regiment (Illus. 2416c).

In the same year, to the *L.-Gds. Finland Regiment*: upper half green, lower black; the same inscription as for the L.-Gds. Izmailovskii Regiment (Illus. 2416d).

In 1814 – The *Guards Équipage* was granted a St.-George flag, completely yellow, with an inscription as for the L.-Gds Preobrazhenii and Semenovskii Regiments (Illus. 2417a).

In 1818 – The *L.-Gds. Lithuania* and *Volhynia* regiments were each granted two St.-George flags, of the same pattern as the preceding and with the inscription: "*Za otlichie pri porazhenii i izgnanii nepriyatelya iz predelov Rossii 1812 goda*". There were differences in the corner colors, which were:

In the Lithuania Regiment—upper half red, lower green (Illus. 2417b).

In the Volhynia Regiment—the entire corner green (Illus. 2417c).

For all four flags, instead of St. George the Bearer of Victory on the eagle's shield, there was an image of a Lithuanian horseman.

In 1824 – A flag was granted to the *L.-Gds. Sapper Battalion*, plain, without an inscription, with black edging along the sides of a yellow cross and with white corners. In the remaining particulars, it was identical to the flags received by the abovementioned Guards regiments in 1814 and 1817 (Illus. 2417d).

e) *Guards Cavalry units.*

Through the year 1814, Guards Cavalry regiments were given standards of the same pattern and colors as confirmed in 1803 for Army Cavalry regiments, namely:

In 1806 – To the *L.-Gds. Horse Regiment* (1 white and 4 green): St.-George flags with the inscription: "*Za vzyatie pri Austerlitse nepriyatel'skago znameni*" [*"For taking an enemy flag at Austerlitz"*].

In 1809 – To the *L.-Gds. Dragoons* (1 white and 4 green): plain, in every corner the inscription: "*S name Bog*" [*"God with us."*] (Illus. 2418).

In 1814 – In the Life-Guards the *Cavalier Guards, Horse, Cuirassier, Dragoon, Hussar,* and *Lancer* regiments were authorized St.-George standards identical to, and in the same numbers as (1 white and 5 green), the St.-George standards received this same year by Army Cavalry regiments, with the following inscriptions: *in the L.-Gds. Horse Regiment*—"*Za vzyatie pri Austerlitse nepriyatel'skago znameni i za otlichie pri porazhenii i izgnanii nepriyatelya iz predelov Rossii 1812 goda*" [*"For taking an enemy flag at Austerlitz and for distinction in the defeat and expulsion of the enemy from Russian territory in 1812"*]; *in the L.-Gds. Lancers*—"*Za vzyatie pri Krasnom nepriyatel'skago znameni i za otlichie pri porazhenii i izgnanii nepriyatelya iz predelov Rossii 1812 goda*" [*"For taking an enemy flag at Krasnyi and for distinction in the defeat and expulsion of the enemy from Russian territory in 1812"*]; and in the remaining regiments—"*Za otlichie pri porazhenii i izgnanii nepriyatelya iz predelov Rossii 1812 goda*"

In 1817 – Instead of the preceding flags, which were never delivered to the regiments, each regiment was granted three of the following St.-George standards with the same inscriptions:

To the *Cavalier Guards Regiment*: yellow with silver, fastened onto a horizontal bar hanging by fine chains from a silver two-headed eagle fixed to the top end of the pole (Illus. 2419).

To the *L.-Gds. Horse*: yellow with silver, with dark-blue [*sinii*] corners; fastened to a bar in the usual manner (Illus. 2421a).

To the *L.-Gds. Dragoons*: yellow with gold, with green corners (Illus. 2421b).

To the *L.-Gds. Hussars*: yellow with gold, with red corners (Illus. 2422a).

To the *L.-Gds. Lancers*: yellow with gold, with dark-blue corners (Illus. 2422b).

The *L.-Gds. Cossacks* were granted three standards, yellow with silver, with dark-blue corners and the inscription: *"Za otlichie pri porazhenii i izgnanii nepriyatelya iz predelov Rossii 1812 goda, i za podvig, okazannyi v srazhenii pri Leiptsige 4 Oktyabrya 1813 goda"* [*"For distinction in the defeat and expulsion of the enemy from Russian territory in 1812, and for the feat performed at the battle of Leipzig, 4 October 1813"*] (Illus. 2423).

In 1818 – The newly formed Life-Guards regiments in Warsaw: *Podolia Cuirassiers*, and *His Imperial Highness the Tsesarevich's* (CONSTANTINE PAVLOVICH'S), were each granted two standards with the inscription: *"Za otlichie pri porazhenii i iznagnii nepriyatelya iz predelov Rossii 1812 goda"* [*"For distinction in the defeat and expulsion of the enemy from Russian territory in 1812"*], and with a Lithuanian horseman on the eagle's breast in place of St. George the Bearer of Victory.

To the *L.-Gds. Podolia* Cuirassier Regiment: similar to the standards of the Cavalier Guards and L.-Gds. Horse Regiment, white with silver, with yellow corners (Illus. 2424a).

To the *L.-Gds. Lancers* of the TSESAREVICH: similar to the rest of the standards in the Guards Cavalry; white with silver, with dark-blue corners (Illus. 2424b).

f) *Military Educational Institutions.*

The *1st Cadet Corps*, during the whole of EMPEROR ALEXANDER I's reign, had flags granted to it during the previous reign: four until 1802, and two since 1802, while since 1814—one, conforming to the rules in effect regarding the number of flags for infantry units of the Guards and Army. In 1806 two of the redundant flags from the 1st Cadet Corps were transferred *to the 2nd Cadet Corps*. In 1810 four flags were granted to the *Nobiliary Regiment*, coming from the number of excess flags prepared for Army regiments in accordance with the design confirmed in 1803: 1 white, 3 with a black cross and red corners. Since 1814 the 1st and 2nd Cadet Corps and each of the Nobiliary Regiment's battalions each were left with only one flag.

Other Military Educational institutions had no flags under EMPEROR ALEXANDER I [131].

▲ *The conquest of Polotsk 6 October 1812*

NOTES

(1) *Complete Collection of Laws* [*Polnoe Sobranie Zakonov*, henceforth PSZ], Vol. XXVI, pg. 609, No. 19,826.

(2) PSZ, Vol. XLIV, pg. 72, No. 19,950, and statements from contemporaries.

(3) From files in the 1st Cadet Corps archive.

(4) Determination by the Military Collegium, 20 October 1803.

(5) PSZ, Vol. XVIII, pg. 415, No. 21,377, and information from contemporaries.

(6) Information from contemporaries.

(7) Actual officers' hats from that time preserved up to now, and information from contemporaries.

(8) PSZ, Vol. XLIV, pg. 67, No. 21,621, and information from contemporaries.

(9) Order of the Director of the 1st Cadet Corps, Major General Klinger.

(10) Order of H.I.H. THE TSESAREVICH CONSTANTINE PAVLOVICH to the 1st Cadet Corps.

(11) Order of the Director of the 1st Cadet Corps, Major General Klinger.

(12) The same order.

(13) PSZ, Vol. XLIV, pg. 14, No. 22,625, and information from contemporaries.

(14) Order of H.I.H. THE TSESAREVICH CONSTANTINE PAVLOVICH to the 1st Cadet Corps.

(15) PSZ, Vol. XLIV, pg. 13, No. 22,727, and information from contemporaries .

(16) Memorandum of the Pavlovsk Cadet Corps to the Staff of HIS IMPERIAL HIGHNESS, the Chief Commander of Military Instructional Institutions, 22 February 1845, No. 363.

(17) PSZ, Vol. XXX, pg. 45, No. 22,784, and information from contemporaries.

(18) Statements from contemporaries.

(19) Order of the Director of the 1st Cadet Corps, Major General Klinger.

(20) From the files of the War Ministry's Commissariat Department.

(21) PSZ, Vol. XLIV, Pt. II, pg. 31, No. 23,377; actual gorgets preserved in the SOVERIEGN EMPEROR's Own Arsenal, and statements from contemporaries.

(22) From the files of the War Ministry's Commissariat Department.

(23) PSZ., Vol. XXX, pg. 970, No. 23,667.

(24) PSZ., Vol. XXX, pg. 1006, No. 23,695.

(25) PSZ, Vol. XLIV, pg. 31, № 23,736.

(26) PSZ, Vol. XXX, pg. 1364/1362, No. 24,049/24019, and statements by contemporaries.

(27) Announcement by the Minister of Military Land Forces to the Director of the 1st Cadet Corps, Major General Kleinmichael, 26 March 1807, No. 946, with an appendix containing a draft outline on the subject of accepting young noblemen into Cadet Corps for military service training.

(28) Announcement by Colonel Kuruta to the Director of the 2nd Cadet Corps, Major General Kleinmichael, 10 July 1810, No. 249.

(29) Statements by contemporaries.

(30) PSZ, Vol. XLIV, pg. 69, No. 24,529, and statements by contemporaries.

(31) PSZ, Vol. XLIV, pg. 69, No. 24,789.

(32) Statements by contemporaries.

(33) Order of the Director of the 1st Cadet Corps, Major General Klinger.

(34) Ditto.

(35) Ditto.

(36) Statements by contemporaries.

(37) From the files of the War Ministry's Commissariat Department, and statements by contemporaries.

(38) HIGHESTOrder, and information from contemporaries.

(39) From files in the 1st Cadet Corps archive.

(40) Information from contemporaries, and shakos preserved up to the present time.

(41) PSZ, Vol. XLIV, pgs. 121 and 122, No. 27,504, and from the files of the War Ministry's Commissariat Department.

(42) Memorandum of the Director of the 1st Moscow Cadet Corps to the Staff of HIS IMPERIAL HIGHNESS , the Chief Commander of Military Instructional Institutions, 27 November 1844, No. 3711.

(43) From the files of the War Ministry's Commissariat Department.

(44) Ditto.

(45) Ditto.

(46) Order of the Chief of HIS IMPERIAL MAJESTY's Main Staff, 10 March 1812, No. 26.

(47) Order to the 1st Cadet Corps by the Chief Director of the Corps of Pages and Cadet Corps, General-Adjutant Golenishchev-Kutuzov.

(48) Ditto.

(49) Information from contemporariesand contemporary drawings.

(50) HIGHESTconfirmed proposal for the formation of the Nobiliary Cavalry Squadron, 28 November 1811.

(51) Information from contemporaries.

(52)Ditto.

(53) Information received from the War Ministry's Commissariat Department.

(54) Information from contemporaries.

(55) PSZ, Vol. XLIV, pg. 101, No. 26,727, and actual pouches preserved from that time.

(56) Ditto.

(57) Information received from the War Ministry's Commissariat Department.

(58) Information from contemporaries.

(59) PSZ, Vol. XXXVII, pg. 409, No. 28,374, and from the files of the War Ministry's Commissariat Department.

(60) Information from contemporaries and drawings from that time.

(61) PSZ, Vol. XXXVI, pg. 396, No. 27,998, §§ 14, 16, and 17.

(62) PSZ, Vol. XLIV, pg. 116, No. 28,264.

(63) *Collection of Laws and Regulations Relating to the Military Administration*, 1822, Book I, pg. 277.

(64) Information from contemporaries and drawings from that time.

(65) PSZ, Vol. XXXVII, pg. 202, No. 28,268, §§ 14 and 16.

(66) *Collection of Laws and Regulations*, 1820, Book II, pg. 387.

(67) Ibid., 1822, Book I, pg. 233.

(68) Information from contemporaries and drawings from that time.

(69) Information obtained from the Corps of Pages by the Headquarters for Military Educational Institutions, 20 March 1845, No. 982, and information from contemporaries.

(70) Ditto.

(71) PSZ, Vol. XLIV, pg. 14, No. 22, 625, and information from contemporaries.

(72) Information from contemporaries.

(73) Ditto.

(74) PSZ, Vol. XXX, pg. 45, No. 22,784, and statements by contemporaries.

(75) PSZ, Vol. XLIV, pg. 73, No. 23,451.

(76) PSZ, Vol. XXX, pg. 1006, No. 23,695, and information from contemporaries.

(77) Information from contemporaries.

(78) PSZ, Vol. XXI, pg. 647, No. 24,625.

(79) Information from contemporaries.

(80) PSZ, Vol. XLIV, pg. 133, No. 25,565.

(81) Information from contemporaries.

(82) PSZ, Vol. XLIV, pg. 138, No. 26,430.

(83) PSZ, Vol. XLIV, pg. 120, No. 26,838.

(84) PSZ, Vol. XLIV, pg. 139, No. 27,560.

(85) PSZ, Vol. XLIV, pg. 119, No. 28,332.

(86) PSZ, Vol. XXXVII, pg. 409, No. 28,374.

(87) PSZ, Vol. XLIV, pg. 140, No. 28,502.

(88) PSZ, Vol. XLIV, pg. 137, No. 30,353.

(89) From the files of the War Ministry's Commissariat Department.

(90) PSZ., Vol. XLIV, pg. 14, No. 22,625, and statements by contemporaries.

(91) From the files of the War Ministry's Commissariat Department.

(92) Information from contemporaries.

(93) From the files of the War Ministry's Commissariat Department.

(94) PSZ, Vol. XXXIII, pg. 451, No. 26,100.

(95) PSZ, Vol. XLIV, pg. 120, No. 26,838.

(96) From the files of the War Ministry's Commissariat Department.

(97) PSZ, Vol. pg. 14, No. 22,625, and information from contemporaries.

(98) From the files of the War Ministry's Commissariat Department.

(99) Statements by contemporaries.

(100) PSZ, Vol. XLIV, pg. 119, No. 28,332.

(101) PSZ, Vol. XXIX, pg. 635, No. 22,214, and from the files of the War Ministry's Commissariat Department.

(102) PSZ, Vol. XLIV, pg. 14, No. 22,625.

(103) Statements by contemporaries.

(104) From the files of the War Ministry's Commissariat Department.

(105) PSZ, Vol. XXXIII, pg. 451, No. 26,100.

(106) From the files of the War Ministry's Commissariat Department.

(107) PSZ, Vol. XLIV, pg. 140, No. 26,480.

(108) PSZ, Vol. XLIV, pg. 120, No. 26,838.

(109) PSZ, Vol. XLIV, pg. 119, No. 28,332.

(110) PSZ, Vol. XLIV, pg. 137, No. 30,353.

(111) PSZ, Vol. XLIV, pg. 139, No. 30,032.

(112) PSZ, Vol. XLIV, pg. 139, No. 30,209.

(113) PSZ, Vol. XL, pg. 208, No. 30,327.

(114) From the files of the War Ministry's Commissariat Department.

(115) PSZ, Vol. XLIV, pg. 139, No. 28,148.

(116) PSZ, Vol. XXVII, pg. 74, No. 183.

(117) PSZ, Vol. XXVII, pg. 372,No. 20,527.

(118).PSZ, Vol. XXXIII, pg. 502,No. 26,147.

(119) PSZ, Vol. XXIX, pg. 1322, No. 22,683.

(120) PSZ, Vol. XLIV, pg. 30, No. 20,186.

(121) PSZ, Vol. XLIV, pg. 108, No. 27,653.

(122) PSZ, Vol. XXVII, pg. 80, No. 20,193.

(123) Announcement of HIS IMPERIAL HIGHNESS , THE TSESAREVICH CONSTANTINE PAVLOVICH to the acting Minister of War, Lieutenant General Gorchakov 1st, 7 August 1814, No. 1851.

(124) Ditto, 31 March 1814, No. 2145.

(125) PSZ, Vol. XXXII, pg. 1083, No. 25,728.

(126) Order of the Chief of HIS IMPERIAL MAJESTY's Main Staff, 25 July 1821, No. 20.

(127) PSZ, Vol. XXIV, pgs. 41 and 68, No. 23,382.

(128) Order of the Chief of HIS IMPERIAL MAJESTY's Main Staff, 17 July 1816.

(129) Ditto, 23 January 1819.

(130) Obtained from the War Ministry's Commissariat Department, and drawings of flags and standards granted during the reign of EMPEROR ALEXANDER I, obtained from regiments.

(131) Information received from the 1st and 2nd Cadet Corps and the Nobiliary Regiment.

РИСУНКИ
ОДЕЖДЫ и ВООРУЖЕНІЯ
РОССІЙСКИХЪ
ВОЙСКЪ
1801-1825.

PLATES LIST OF ILLUSTRATIONS

2354. Officer Candidate [*Yunker*] and Company-Grade Officer. Artillery School, 1820-1822.

2355. Shako plate, Main Engineering School, established 24 November 1819.

2356. Officer Candidate [*Yunker*]. Artillery School, 1822-1824.

2357. Company-Grade Officer. Artillery School, 1824.

2358. Page and Chamber Page. Corps of Pages, 1802-1807.

2359. Field-Grade Officer. Corps of Pages, 1802-1804.

2360. Officers' coat embroidery for the Corps of Pages, established in 1808.

2361. Company-Grade Officer and Chamber Page. Corps of Pages, 1807-1810.

2362. Page and Field-Grade Officer. Corps of Pages, 1812-1825.

2363. Infantry General. 1808-1810.

2364. Standard generals' coat embroidery, established 26 January 1808.

2365. Garrison General. 1809-1810.

2366. Cavalry General. 1814-1825. (Light Cavalry.)

2367. Cavalry General. 1814-1825. (Heavy Cavalry.)

2368. Garrison General. 1816-1820.

2369. Infantry General. 1817-1825.

2370. Garrison General. 1820-1825.

2371. General. Separate Lithuania Corps, 1825.

2372. General. Separate Lithuania Corps, 1825.

2373. Infantry General Adjutant [*General-Ad"yutant*]. 1802-1804.

2374. Cavalry Aide-de-Camp [*Fligel'-Ad"yutant*]. 1802-1804.

2375. Cavalry General Adjutant. 1807-1812.

2376. General-Adjutants' coat embroidery, established in 1815.

2377. General-Adjutant's epaulette, established in 1815.

2378. Cavalry General Adjutant. 1814-1825. (Heavy Cavalry.)

2379. Cavalry Aide-de-Camp. 1814-1825. (Light Cavalry.)

2380. Field-Grade Officer, in the Army at large. 1802-1804.

2381. Company-Grade Officer, in the Cavalry at large. 1807-1810.

2382. Field-Grade Officer, in the Army at large. 1812-1825.

2383. Guards Cavalry Adjutant. 1815-1825. (Heavy Cavalry.)

2384. Army Cavalry Adjutant. 1815-1825. (Light Cavalry.)

2385. Guards Cavalry Adjutant. 1815-1825. (Light Cavalry.)

2386. Coat embroidery for Guards adjutants, established in 1815.

2387. Army Infantry Staff Duty Officer, 1815-1817.

2388. Adjutant. Separate Corps of the Internal Guard, 1816-1825.

2389. Army Infantry Staff Duty Officer, 1817-1825.

2390. Guards Infantry Adjutant. 1817-1825.

2391. Adjutant and Staff Duty Officer. Separate Lithuania Corps, 1825.

2392. Army Infantry Town Major. 1824-1825.

2393. Guards Infantry Town Adjutant. 1825.

2394. Wagonmaster-General. 1816-1825.

2395. Provost-General. 1816-1825.

2396. Army Senior Wagonmaster. 1816-1825.

2397. Guards Senior Provost. 1816-1825.

2398. Guards and Army Orderlies. 1802-1812.

2399. Guards and Army Orderlies. 1819-1825.

2400. White flag, established in 1803 for Grenadier and Musketeer (Infantry since 1811) regiments.

2401. Flags for Army infantry. 1803-1815.

2402. Flags for Army infantry, 1803-1815.

2403. Flags granted to Army infantry regiments. a. Moscow Grenadiers, 1804. b. Kiev Grenadiers, 1807. c. Villmanstrand, Brest, Kremenchug, and Minsk Musketeers, 1807. c. Belostok Musketeers, 1808.

2404. Flags granted to Army infantry regiments. a. Pernau Musketeers. b. Schlüsselburg Musketeers. c. Azov Musketeers. c. Phanagoria Grenadiers, 1808.

2405. Flags granted to Army infantry regiments. a. Narva Musketeers, 1810. b. Dnieper Musketeers, 1810. c. Georgia Grenadiers, 1812. d. Vilna Infantry, 1812.

2406. Flags granted to Army infantry regiments in 1812. a. Tarnopol. b. Simbirsk. c. Perm.

2407. Flags for Army regiments, 1816-1825. a. Regiments of the 1st Grenadier Division. b. Regiments of the 2nd Grenadier Division. c. Regiments of the 3rd Grenadier Division. d. Marine Infantry regiments.

2408. Standards for cavalry regiments, 1803-1815.

2409. Standards for cavalry regiments, 1805-1815.

2410. Flags granted to Garrison battalions in 1805. a. Vilna, Minsk, and Grodno. b. Yekaterinoslav. c. Vladika-vkaz. d. Kamenets-Podolia.

2411. Flags granted to Garrison battalions. a. Vologda and Velikii-Ustyug Battalions, 1805, and Penza Battalion, 1807. b. Ufa Battalion, 1808. c. Sveaborg Regiment, 1810.

2412. Flags proposed to be granted to Guards infantry regiments, 1813. a. L.-Gds. Preobrazhenskii. b. L.-Gds. Semenovskii. c. L.-Gds. Izmailovskii. d. L.-Gds. Jägers.

2413 and 2414. Flags proposed to be granted to Guards infantry regiments, 1813. a. and b. L.-Gds. Lithuania. c. L.-Gds. Grenadiers. d. L.-Gds. Pavlovsk. e. L.-Gds. Finland.

2415. Flags granted to Guards infantry regiments, 1814. a. L.-Gds. Preobrazhenskii. b. L.-Gds. Semenovskii. c. L.-Gds. Izmailovskii. d. L.-Gds. Jägers.

2416. Flags granted to Guards infantry regiments, 1817. a. L.-Gds. Lithuania (later L.-Gds. Moscow). b. L.-Gds. Grenadiers. c. L.-Gds. Pavlovsk. d. L.-Gds. Finland.

2417. Flags granted to Guards infantry units, 1817. a. Guards Équipage, 1817. b. L.-Gds. Lithuania Regiment, 1818. c. L.-Gds. Volhynia Regiment, 1818. d. L.-Gds. Sapper Battalion, 1824.

2418. Standards of the L.-Gds. Dragoon Regiment, granted in 1810.

2419. Standard of the Cavalier Guards Regiment, established in 1817.

2420. Standard of the L.-Gds. Horse Regiment, granted in 1817.

2421 & 2422. Standards granted to Life-Guards reg. in 1817. a. Cuirassiers. b. Dragoons., c. Hussars. d. Lancers.

2423. Standard granted to the L.-Gds. Cossack Regiment, 1817.

2424. Standards granted to Life-Guards regiments in 1818. a. Podolia Cuirassiers. b. The Tsesarevich's Lancers.

Musketeer and Grenader. 1st Cadet Corps, 1802-1804.

Grenadier and Grenadier Non-Commissioned Officer. 2nd Cadet Corps, 1802-1804

Musketeer Non-Commissione2d Officer. 1st Cadet Corps, 1802-1804

Company-Grade Officers. 1st and 2nd Cadet Corps, 1802-1804

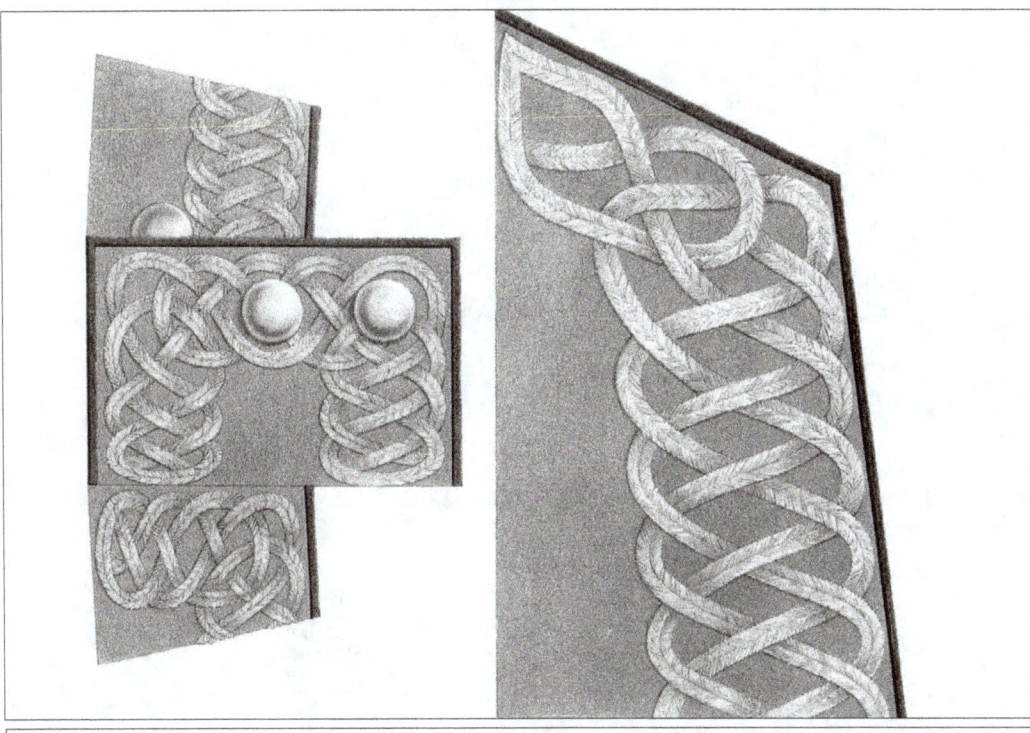

Officers' coat embroidery for the 1st and 2nd Cadet Corps, established in 1802
Shako plate of the 1st and 2nd Cadet Corps and Nobiliary Regiment, established in 1810

Cadets. Young Boys' Section of the 1st Cadet Corps, 1802-1813

Drummer of the 1st Cadet Corps and Fifer of the 2nd Cadet Corps, 1802-1804.

Musketeers. 1st and 2nd Cadet Corps, 1804-1807

Grenadier. 2nd Cadet Corps, 1803-1805

Field-Grade Officer of the 1st Cadet Corps and Company-Grade Officer of the 2nd Cadet Corps, 1807-1810

Musketeer of the 1st Cadet Corps and Grenadier of the 2nd Cadet Corps, 1807-1809

Grenadier. 2nd Cadet Corps, 1808-1810

Musketeer and Company-Grade Officer. 2nd Cadet Corps, 1809

Company-Grade Officer, Musketeer, and Grenadier. Nobiliary Battalions, 1809

Musketeer Non-Commissioned Officer. Nobiliary Regiment, 1810-1811

Grenadier of the 1st Cadet Corps and Company-Grade Officer of the 2nd Cadet Corps, 1810

Grenadier Non-Commissioned Officer, Musketeer, and Marksman [Strelok]. 1st Cadet Corps, 1811

Cadet. 2nd Cadet Corps, 1811

Grenadiers. 1st Cadet Corps and Nobiliary Regiment, 1812-1817

Company-Grade Officers. 2nd Cadet Corps and Nobiliary Regiment, 1812-1817

Musician. 2nd Cadet Corps, 1814-1820

Marksman of the 1st Cadet Corps and Company-Grade Officer of the Imperial Military Orphans Home, 1817-1820

Hornist. Nobiliary Regiment, 1819-1820

Drummer. 1st Cadet Corps, 1820-1824

Musketeer of the 1st Cadet Corps and Musketeer Company-Grade Officer of the Nobiliary Regiment, 1822-1824

Cadet. Moscow Cadet Corps, 1824-1825

Company-Grade Officer and Non-Commissioned Officer of the 2nd Cadet Corps and Cadet of the Imperial Military Orphans Home, 1824

Noble. Nobiliary Cavalry Squadron, 1811

Noble. Nobiliary Cavalry Squadron, 1816-1818

Noble. Nobiliary Cavalry Squadron, 1816-1818

Noble and Company-Grade Officer. Nobiliary Cavalry Squadron, 1818-1824

Cadets [Konduktory] and Company-Grade Officer. Main Engineering School, 1819-1820

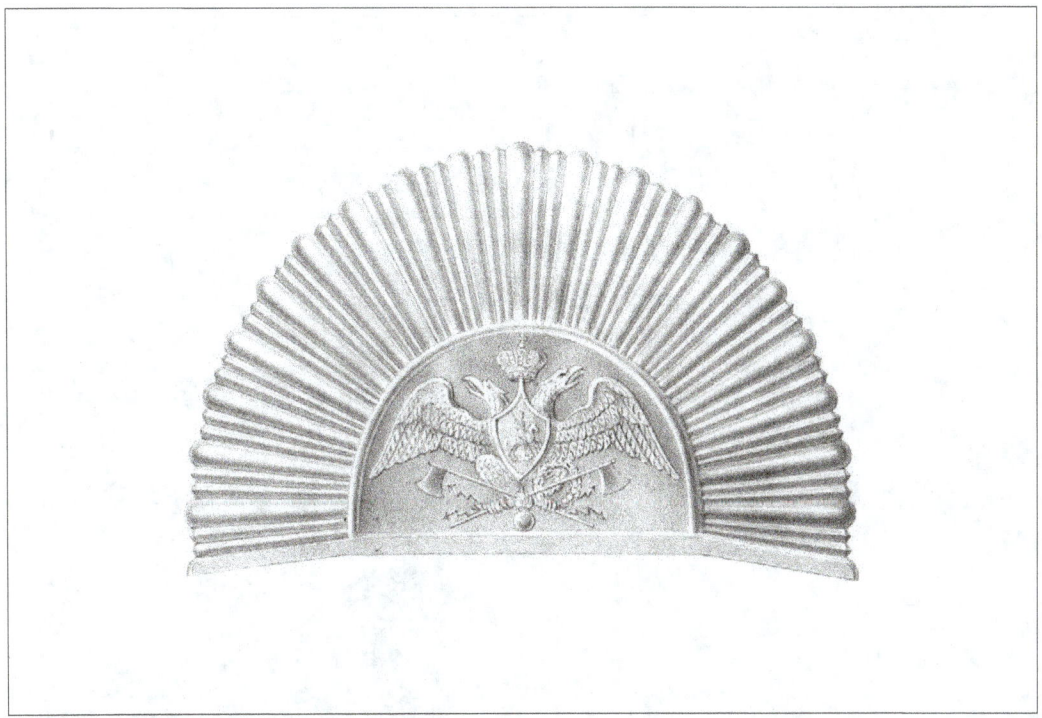

Shako plate, Artillery School, established 9 May 1820
Shako plate, Main Engineering School, established 24 November 1819

Cadet [Konduktor]. Main Engineering School, 1820-1822

Company-Grade Officer and Cadet [Konduktor]. Main Engineering School, 1822-1824

Cadet [Konduktor]. Main Engineering School, 1824-1825

Officer Candidate [Yunker] and Company-Grade Officer. Artillery School, 1820-1822

Officer Candidate [Yunker]. Artillery School, 1822-1824

Officer Candidate [Yunker]. Artillery School, 1822-1824

Page and Chamber Page. Corps of Pages, 1802-1807

Field-Grade Officer. Corps of Pages, 1802-1804

Officers' coat embroidery for the Corps of Pages, established in 1808

Standard generals' coat embroidery, established 26 January 1808

Company-Grade Officer and Chamber Page. Corps of Pages, 1807-1810

Page and Field-Grade Officer. Corps of Pages, 1812-1825

Infantry General. 1808-1810

Garrison General. 1809-1810.

Cavalry General. 1814-1825. (Light Cavalry.)

Cavalry General. 1814-1825. (Heavy Cavalry.)

2368

Garrison General. 1816-1820

Infantry General. 1817-1825

Garrison General. 1820-1825

General. Separate Lithuania Corps, 1825

General. Separate Lithuania Corps, 1825

Infantry General Adjutant [General-Ad'yutant]. 1802-1804.

2374

Cavalry Aide-de-Camp [Fligel-Adyutant]. 1802-1804

Cavalry General Adjutant. 1807-1812

General-Adjutants' coat embroidery, established in 1815

General-Adjutant's epaulette, established in 1815

Cavalry General Adjutant. 1814-1825. (Heavy Cavalry.)

Cavalry Aide-de-Camp. 1814-1825. (Light Cavalry.)

Field-Grade Officer, in the Army at large. 1802-1804

Company-Grade Officer, in the Cavalry at large. 1807-1810

Field-Grade Officer, in the Army at large. 1812-1825

Guards Cavalry Adjutant. 1815-1825. (Heavy Cavalry.)

Army Cavalry Adjutant. 1815-1825. (Light Cavalry.)

Guards Cavalry Adjutant. 1815-1825. (Light Cavalry)

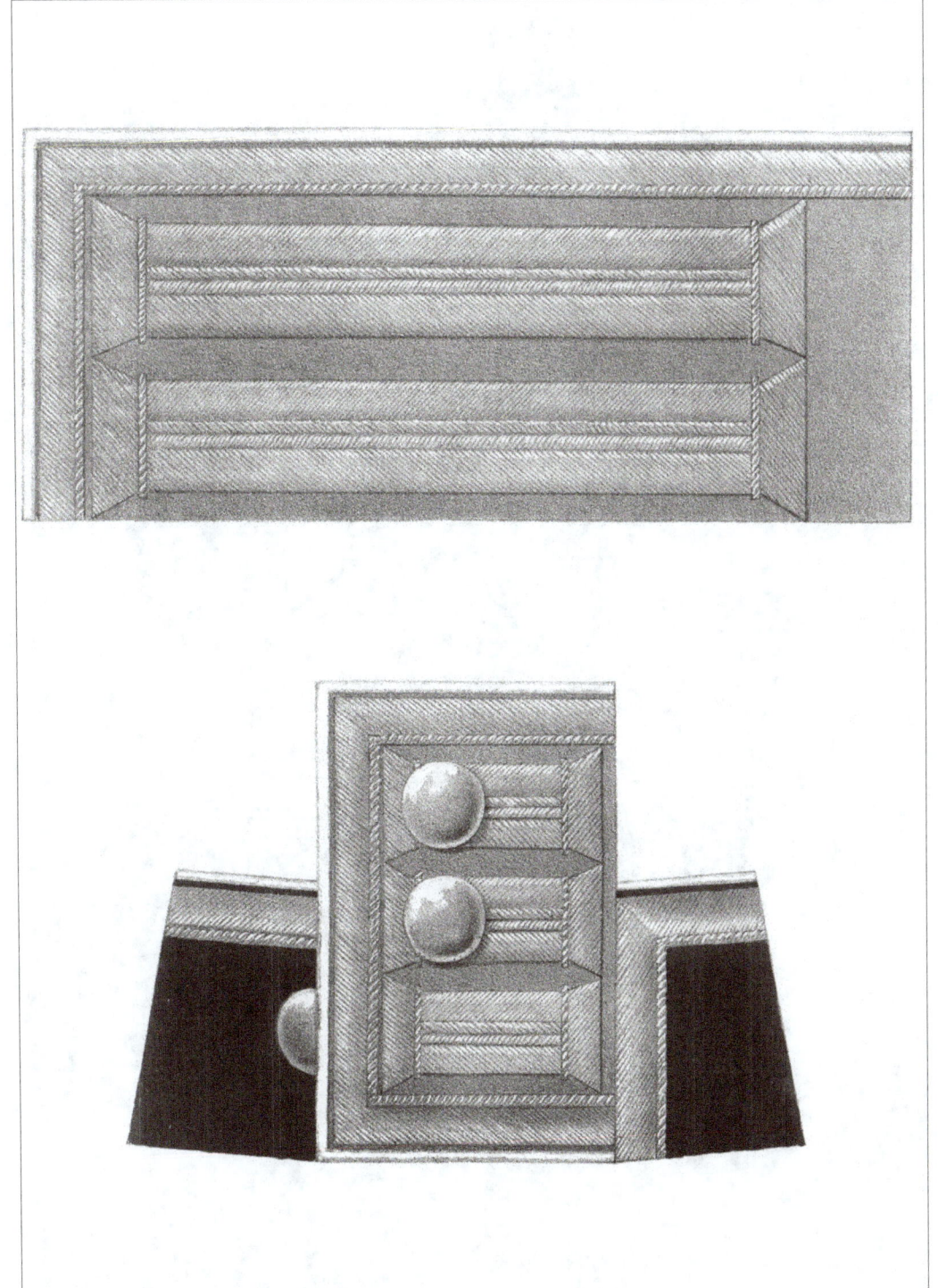

Coat embroidery for Guards adjutants, established in 1815

Army Infantry Staff Duty Officer, 1815-1817

Adjutant. Separate Corps of the Internal Guard, 1816-1825

Army Infantry Staff Duty Officer, 1817-1825

Guards Infantry Adjutant. 1817-1825

Adjutant and Staff Duty Officer. Separate Lithuania Corps, 1825

Army Infantry Town Major. 1824-1825

Guards Infantry Town Adjutant. 1825

Wagonmaster-General. 1816-1825

Provost-General. 1816-1825.

Army Senior Wagonmaster. 1816-1825

Guards Senior Provost. 1816-1825

Guards and Army Orderlies. 1802-1812

Guards and Army Orderlies. 1819-1825

White flag, established in 1803 for Grenadier and Musketeer (Infantry since 1811) reg. - Standard granted to the L.-Gds. Cossack Reg. 1817

Flags for Army infantry. 1803-1815

Flags for Army infantry, 1803-1815

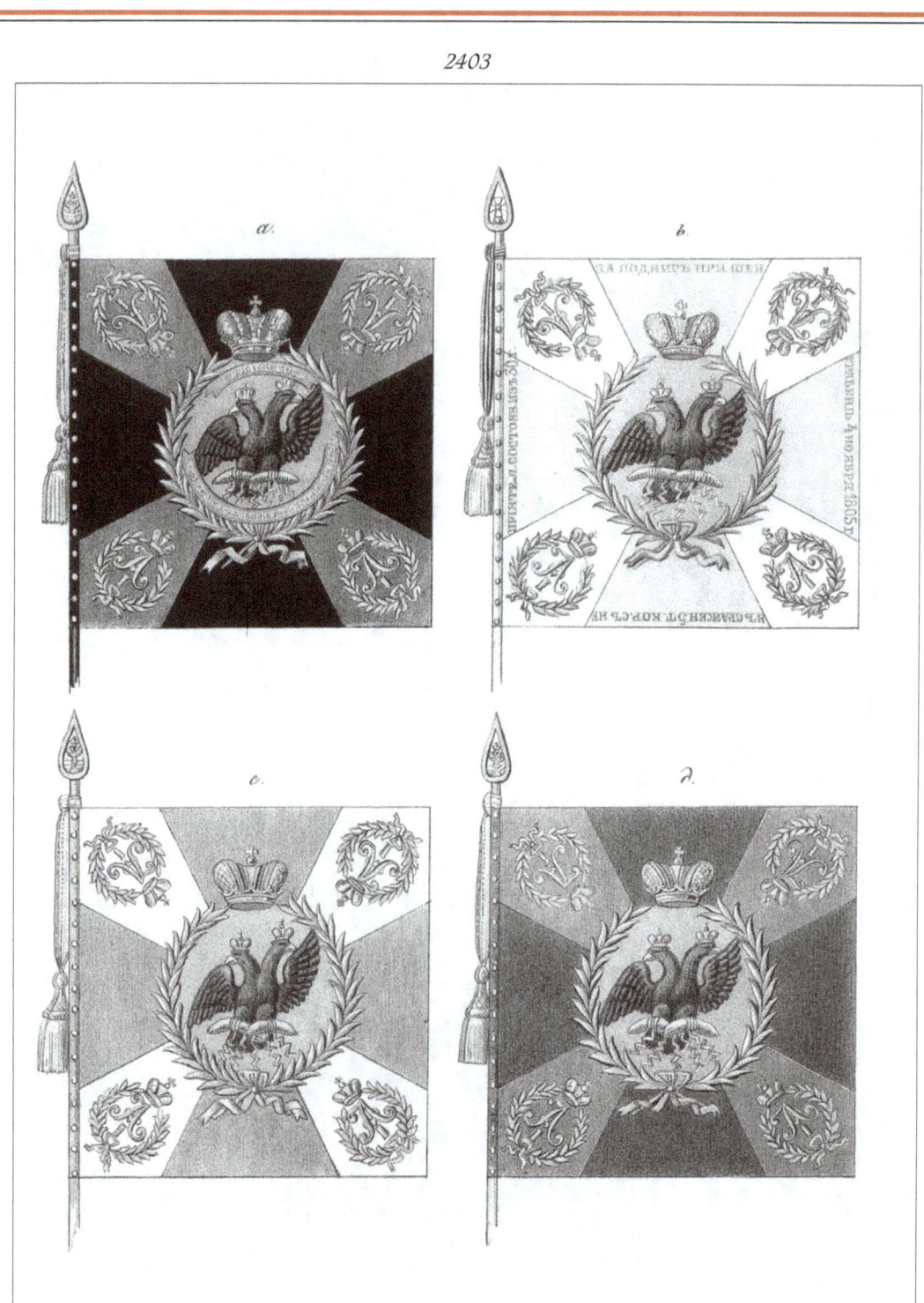

Flags granted to Army infantry regiments. a. Moscow Grenadiers, 1804. b. Kiev Grenadiers, 1807. c. Villmanstrand, Brest, Kremenchug, and Minsk Musketeers, 1807. c. Belostok Musketeers, 1808.

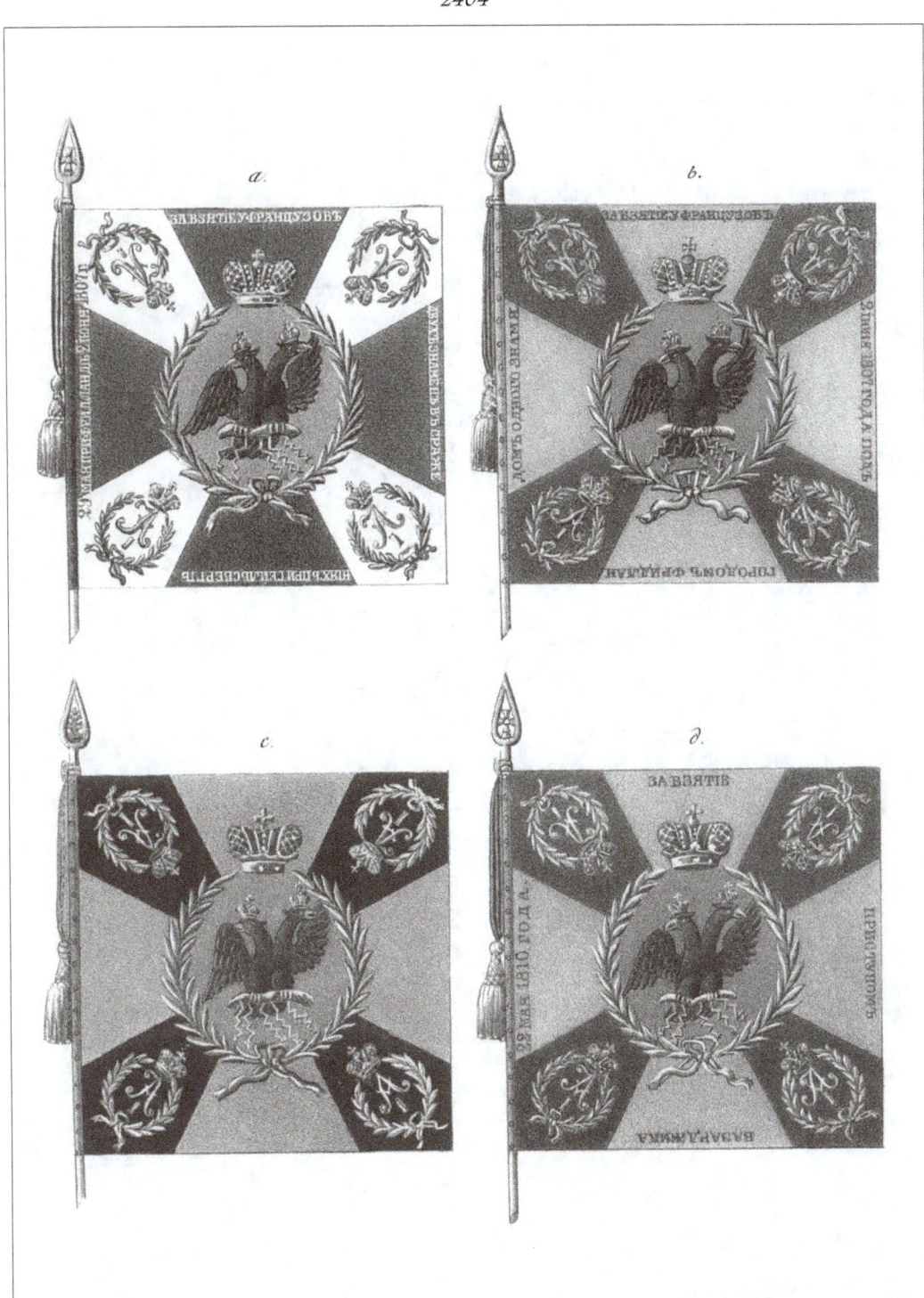

Flags granted to Army infantry regiments. a. Pernau Musketeers. b. Schlüsselburg Musketeers. c. Azov Musketeers. c. Phanagoria Grenadiers, 1808

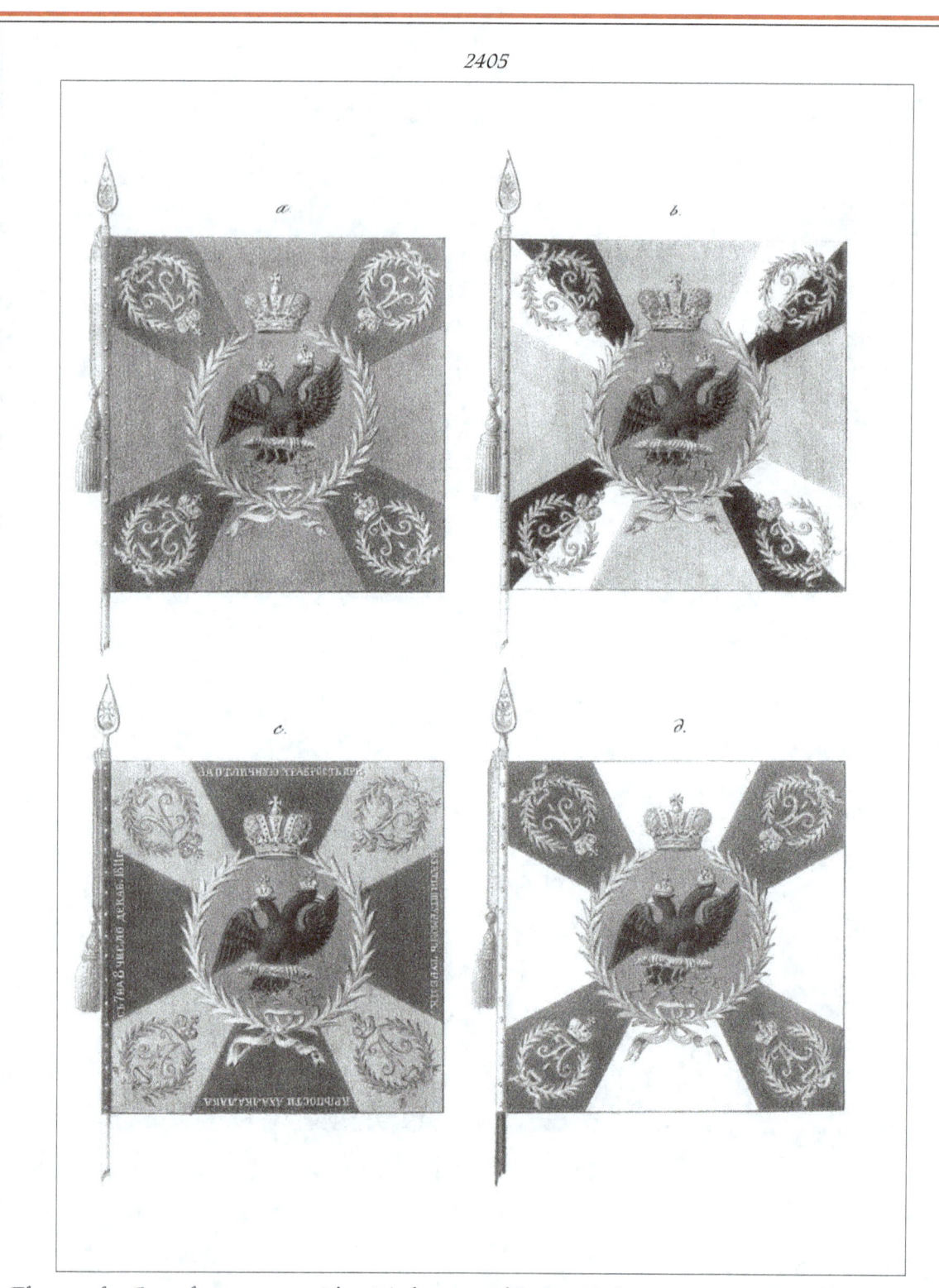

Flags granted to Army infantry regiments. a. Narva Musketeers, 1810. b. Dnieper Musketeers, 1810. c. Georgia Grenadiers, 1812. d. Vilna Infantry, 1812.

Flags granted to Army infantry regiments in 1812. a. Tarnopol. b. Simbirsk. c. Perm.

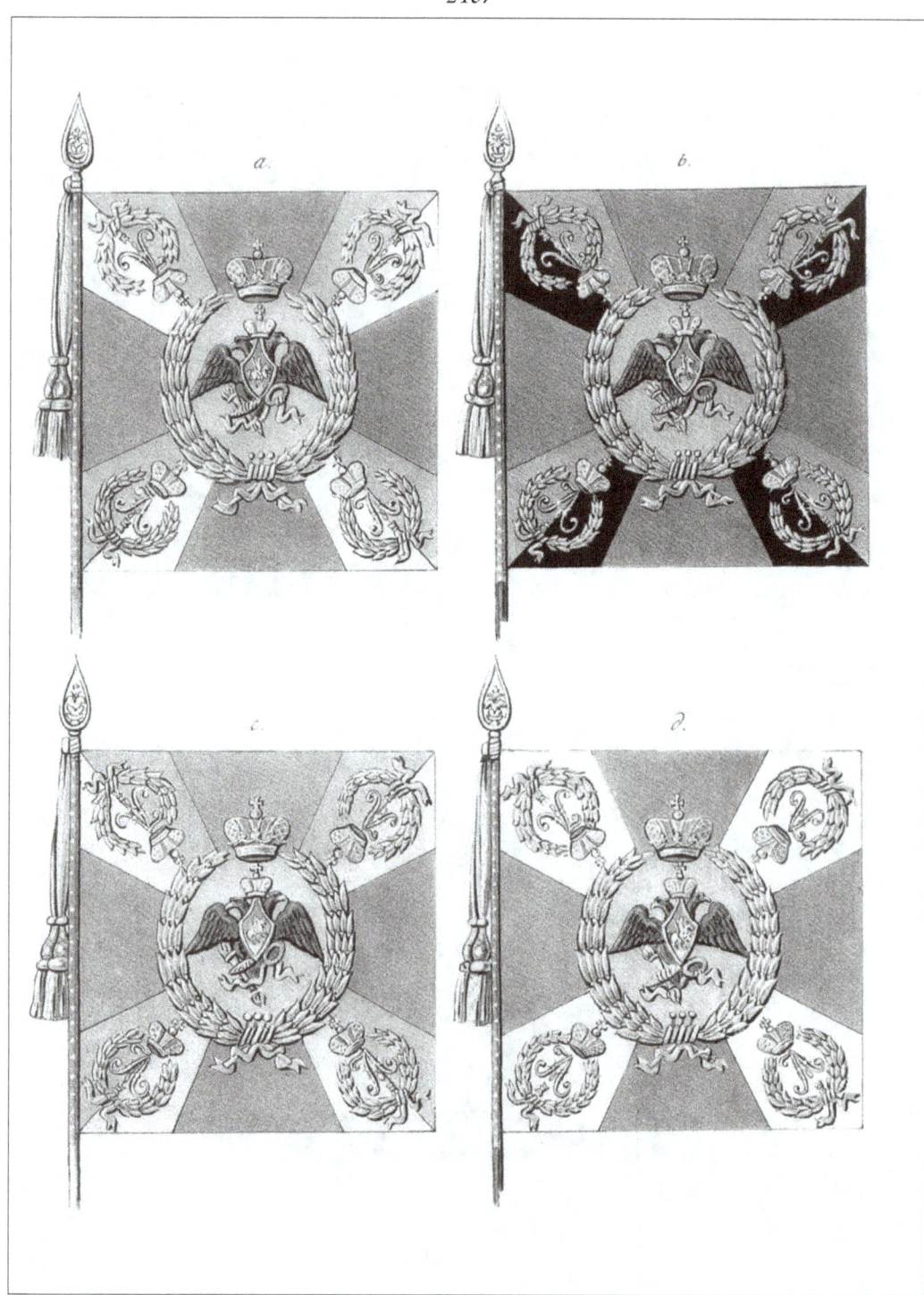

Flags for Army regiments, 1816-1825. a. Regiments of the 1st Grenadier Division. b. Regiments of the 2nd Grenadier Division. c. Regiments of the 3rd Grenadier Division. d. Marine Infantry regiments

Standards for cavalry regiments, 1803-1815 - Standards for cavalry regiments, 1805-1815

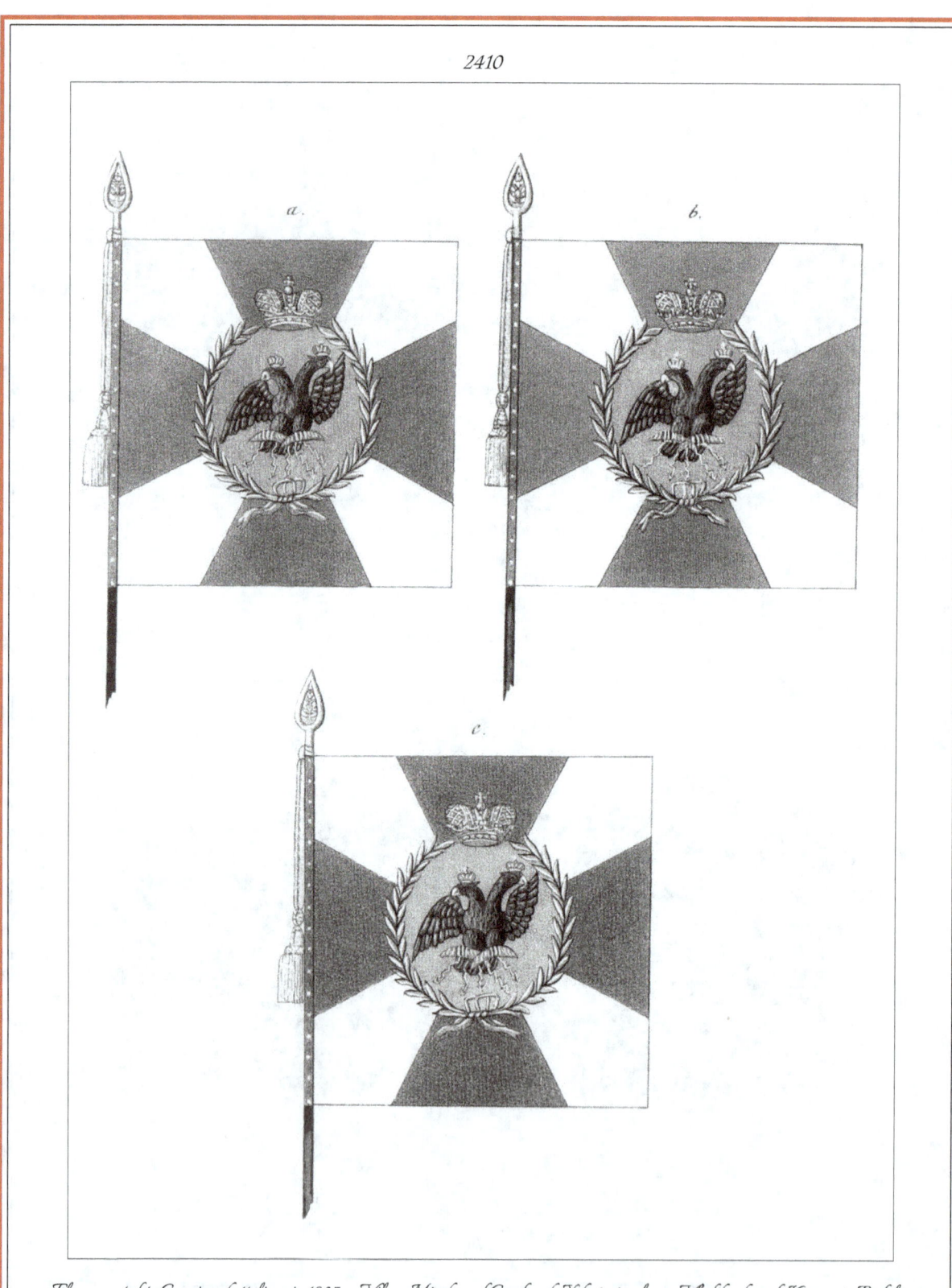

Flags granted to Garrison battalions in 1805. a. Vilna, Minsk, and Grodno. b. Yekaterinoslav. c. Vladikavkaz. d. Kamenets-Podolia

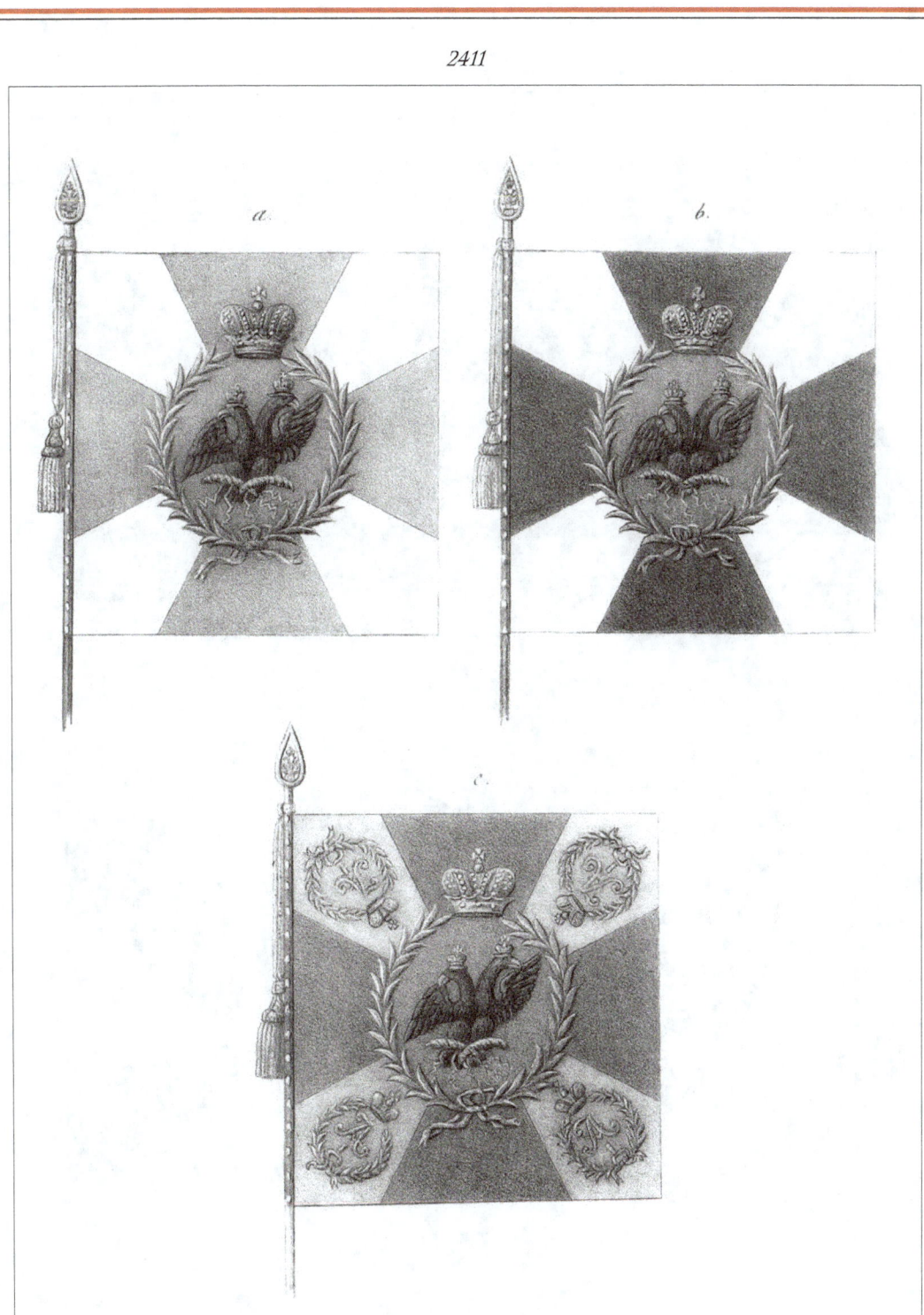

Flags granted to Garrison battalions. a. Vologda and Velikii-Ustyug Battalions, 1805, and Penza Battalion, 1807. b. Ufa Battalion, 1808. c. Sveaborg Regiment, 1810

Flags proposed to be granted to Guards infantry regiments, 1813. a. L.-Gds. Preobrazhenskii. b. L.-Gds. Semenovskii. c. L.-Gds. Izmailovskii. d. L.-Gds. Jägers.

Flags proposed to be granted to Guards infantry regiments, 1813. a. and b. L.-Gds. Lithuania. c. L.-Gds. Grenadiers. d. L.-Gds. Pavlovsk. e. L.-Gds. Finland

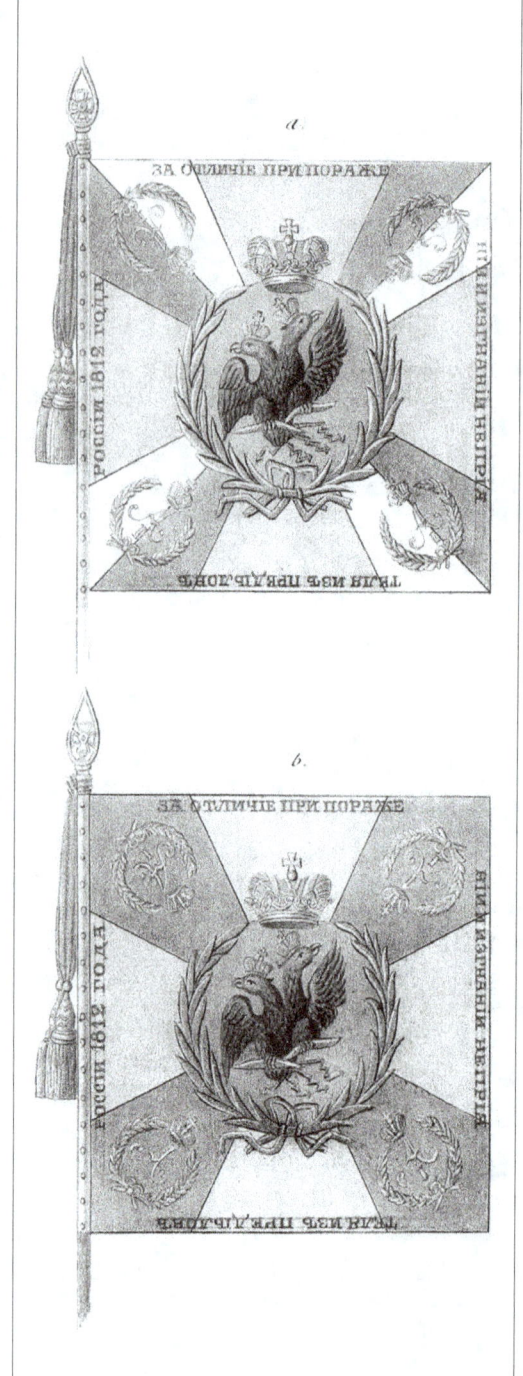

Flags proposed to be granted to Guards infantry regiments, 1813. a. and b. L.-Gds. Lithuania. c. L.-Gds. Grenadiers. d. L.-Gds. Pavlovsk. e. L.-Gds. Finland - Standard of the Cavalier Guards Regiment, established in 1817 - Standard of the L.-Gds. Horse Regiment, granted in 1817

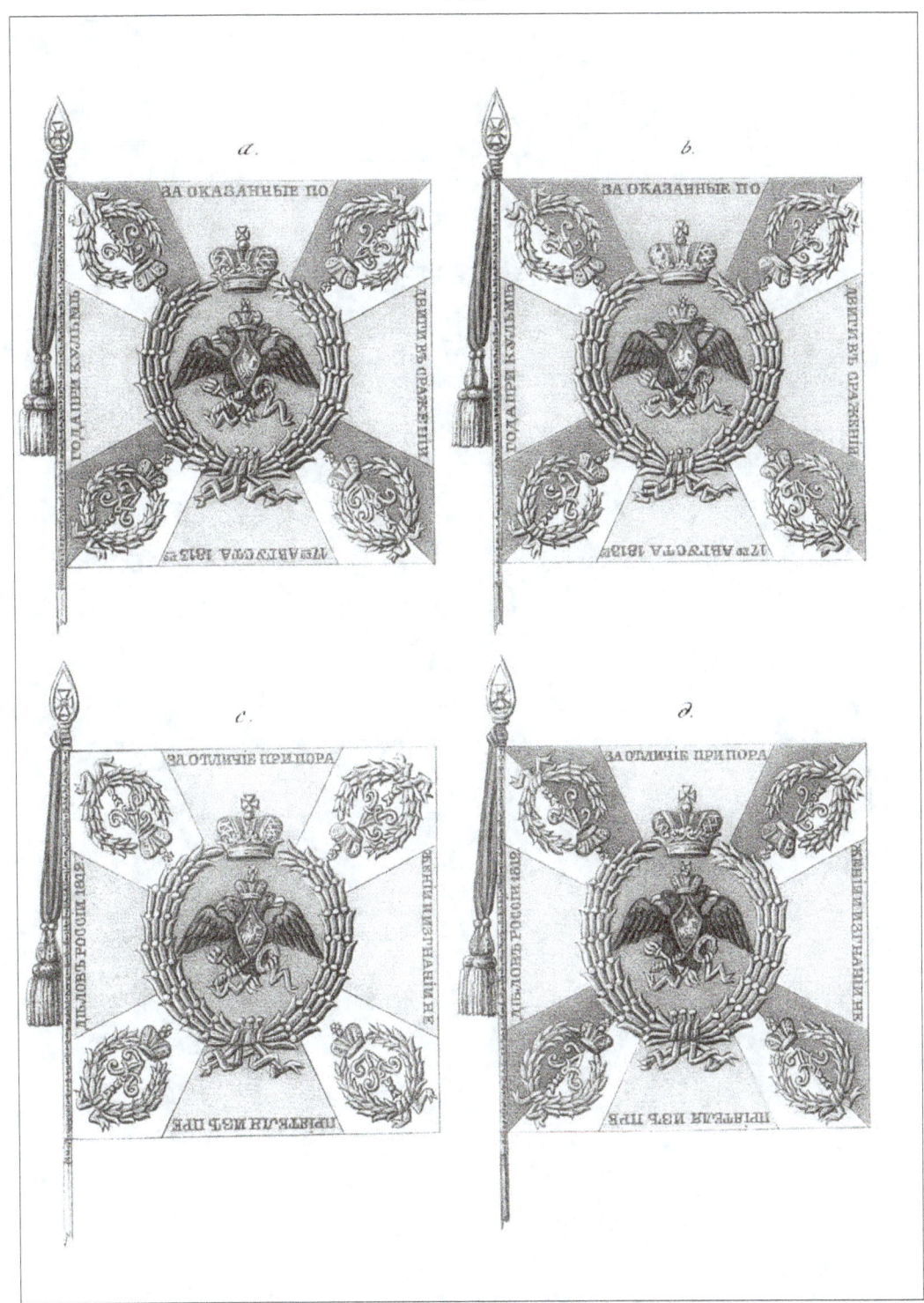

Flags granted to Guards infantry regiments, 1814. a. L.-Gds. Preobrazhenskii. b. L.-Gds. Semenovskii. c. L.-Gds. Izmailovskii. d. L.-Gds. Jägers

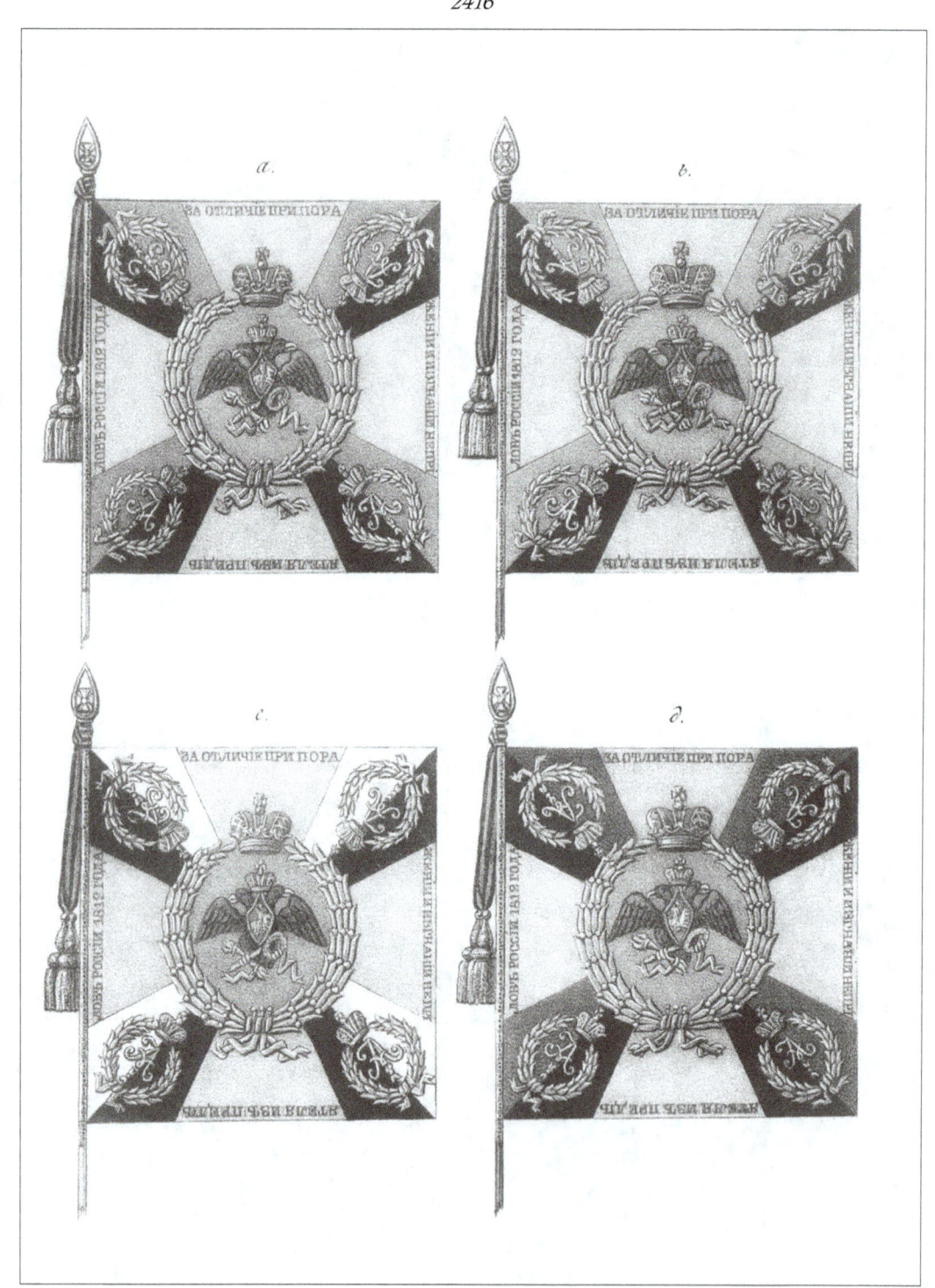

Flags granted to Guards infantry regiments, 1817. a. L.-Gds. Lithuania (later L.-Gds. Moscow). b. L.-Gds. Grenadiers. c. L.-Gds. Pavlovsk. d. L.-Gds. Finland

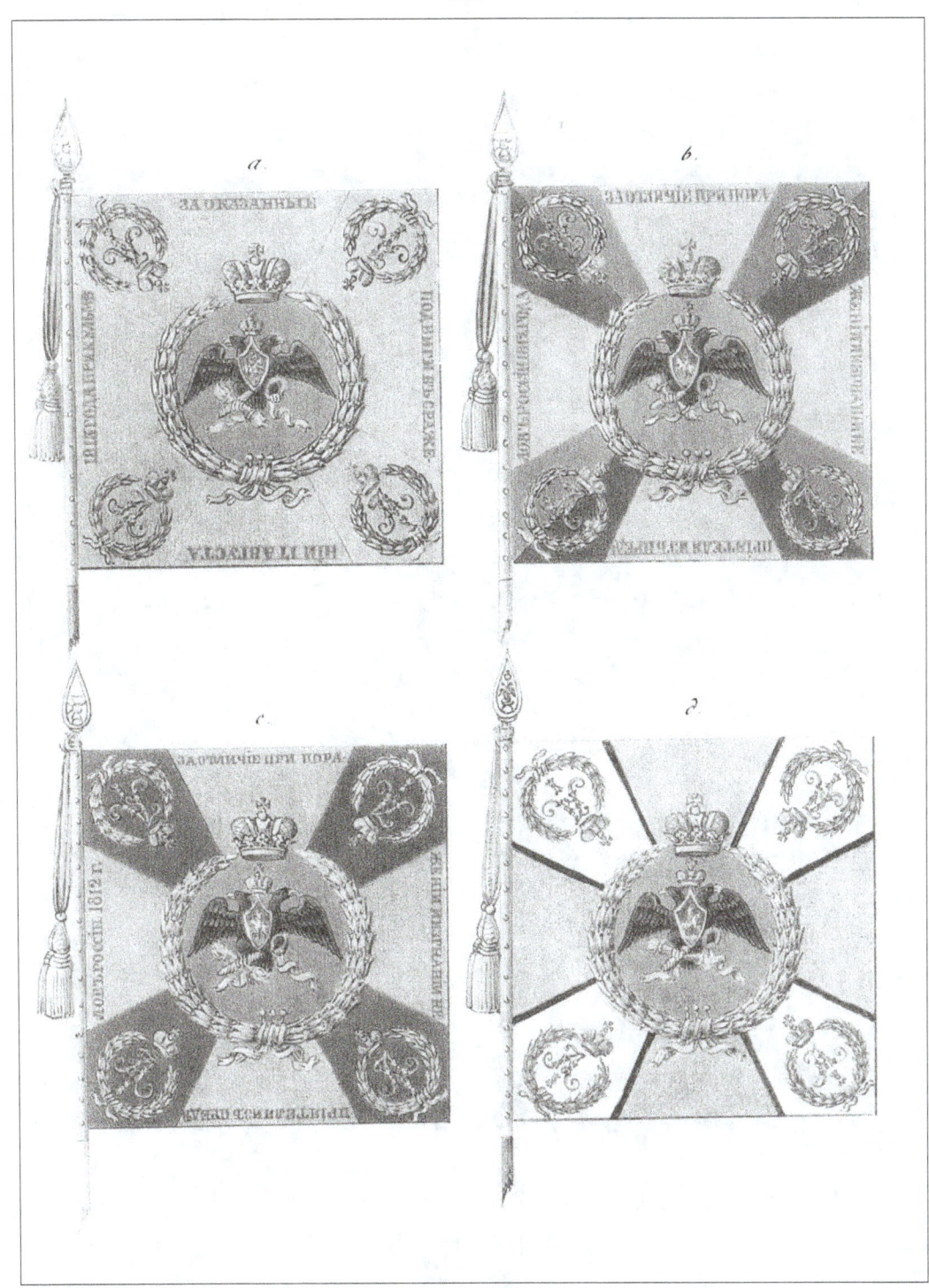

Flags granted to Guards infantry units, 1817. a. Guards Équipage, 1817. b. L.-Gds. Lithuania Regiment, 1818. c. L.-Gds. Volhynia Regiment, 1818. d. L.-Gds. Sapper Battalion, 1824

Standards of the L.-Gds. Dragoon Regiment, granted in 1810 - Standards granted to Life-Guards regiments in 1817. a. Cuirassiers. b. Dragoons., c. Hussars. d. Lancers

Standards granted to Life-Guards regiments in 1817. a. Cuirassiers. b. Dragoons., c. Hussars. d. Lancers
Standards granted to Life-Guards regiments in 1818. a. Podolia Cuirassiers. b. The Tsesarevich's Lancers

SOLDIERS, WEAPONS & UNIFORMS ALREADY PUBLISHED
(SOME TITLES)

UNIFORMS OF RUSSIAN ARMY IN THE ERA OF ANCIENT TZAR
FROM THE REIGN OF VASILI IV TO MICHAEL I, ALEXIS, FEODOR III DURING THE XVII th CENTURY
A.V.VISKOVATOV — LUCA STEFANO CRISTINI
SWU-600-004

UNIFORMS OF RUSSIAN ARMY OF PETER I THE GREAT
FROM THE REIGN OF PETER I TO CATHERINE I, PEER II, ANNA AND IVAN VI, 1682-1741
A.V.VISKOVATOV — LUCA STEFANO CRISTINI
SWU-700-006

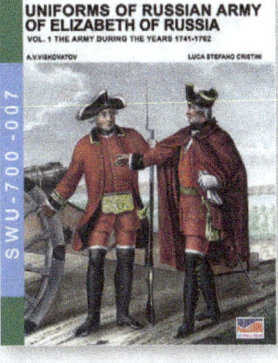

UNIFORMS OF RUSSIAN ARMY OF ELIZABETH OF RUSSIA
VOL. 1 THE ARMY DURING THE YEARS 1741-1762
A.V.VISKOVATOV — LUCA STEFANO CRISTINI
SWU-700-007

UNIFORMS OF RUSSIAN ARMY OF ELIZABETH OF RUSSIA
VOL. 2 THE ARMY DURING THE YEARS 1741-1762
A.V.VISKOVATOV — LUCA STEFANO CRISTINI
SWU-700-008

UNIFORMS OF RUSSIAN ARMY IN THE XVIII CENTURY VOL. 1
UNDER THE REIGN OF CATHERINE II EMPRESS OF RUSSIA BETWEEN 1762 AND 1796
A.V.VISKOVATOV – LUCA STEFANO CRISTINI
SWU-700-005

UNIFORMS OF RUSSIAN ARMY IN THE XVIII CENTURY VOL. 2
UNDER THE REIGN OF CATHERINE II EMPRESS OF RUSSIA BETWEEN 1762 AND 1796
A.V.VISKOVATOV – LUCA STEFANO CRISTINI
SWU-700-009

UNIFORMS OF RUSSIAN ARMY IN THE XVIII CENTURY VOL. 3
UNDER THE REIGN OF CATHERINE II EMPRESS OF RUSSIA BETWEEN 1762 AND 1796
A.V.VISKOVATOV – LUCA STEFANO CRISTINI
SWU-700-010

UNIFORMS OF RUSSIAN ARMY IN THE XVIII CENTURY VOL. 4
UNDER THE REIGN OF CATHERINE II EMPRESS OF RUSSIA BETWEEN 1762 AND 1796
A.V.VISKOVATOV – LUCA STEFANO CRISTINI
SWU-700-011

BRITISH ARMY UNIFORMS IN 1742
IN THE ART OF JOHN PINE
SWU-700-001

PRUSSIAN & AUSTRIAN ARMY UNIFORMS IN 1742-1770
LUCA STEFANO CRISTINI
SWU-700-002

THE FRENCH ARMY OF ANCIEN RÉGIME Volume 1
IN THE ART OF FELIX PHILIPPOTEAUX
LUCA STEFANO CRISTINI
SWU-700-003

THE FRENCH ARMY OF ANCIEN RÉGIME Volume 2
IN THE ART OF FELIX PHILIPPOTEAUX
LUCA STEFANO CRISTINI
SWU-700-004

THE EXERCISE OF ARMES
JACOB DE GHEYN II – LUCA S. CRISTINI
SWU-600-001

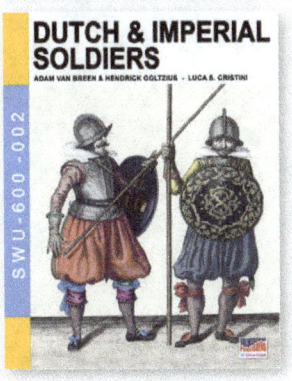

DUTCH & IMPERIAL SOLDIERS
ADAM VAN BREEN & HENDRICK GOLTZIUS – LUCA S. CRISTINI
SWU-600-002

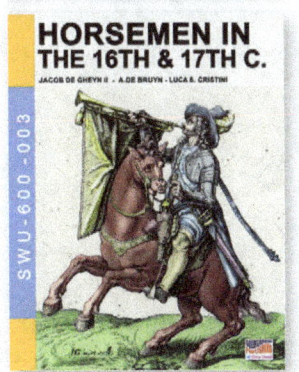

HORSEMEN IN THE 16TH & 17TH C.
JACOB DE GHEYN II – A.DE BRUYN – LUCA S. CRISTINI
SWU-600-003

IMPERIAL SOLDIERS & UNIFORMS 1640-1860
IN THE ART OF FRANZ GERASCH
LUCA S. CRISTINI
Plates by FRANZ GERASCH
SWU-GEN-001

133